Images of Modern America

BARTLETT ARBORETUM & GARDENS

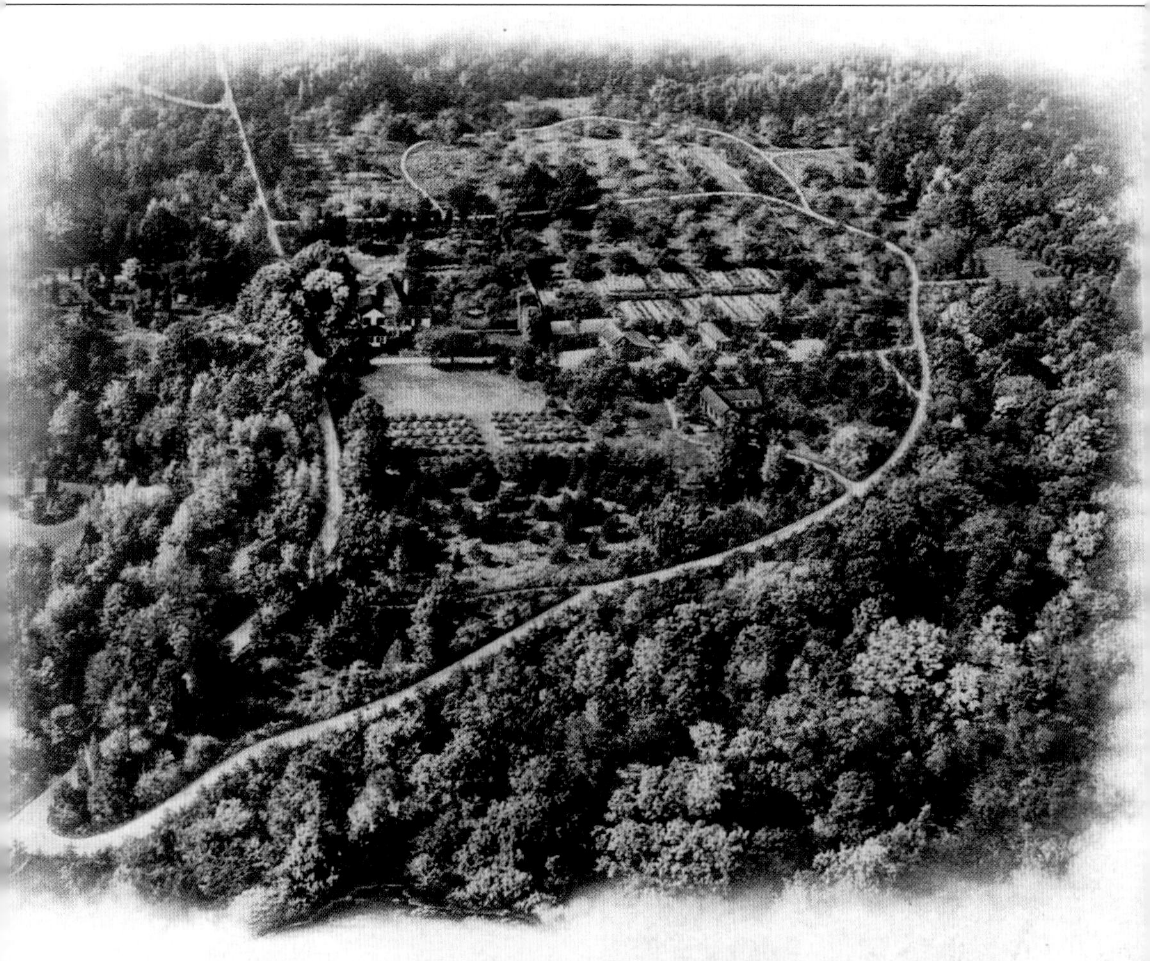

Bartlett Tree Research Laboratories. In 1963, at the time of Francis Bartlett's death, the Bartlett Tree Research Laboratories encompassed nearly 200 acres of property in North Stamford, Connecticut. This rendering shows the scope of the property at its peak before sales of lots reduced the acreage to 64, and it was bought by the State of Connecticut, which renamed it the Bartlett Arboretum in 1966. (Courtesy of The F.A. Bartlett Tree Expert Company.)

Front Cover: The arboretum is captivating in all seasons as depicted by this autumn image of the bridge over Poorhouse Brook on the Red Oak Trail. (Courtesy of Ed vanVeen, Edward V. Photography.)

Upper Back Cover: Forsyth Pond features a spillway, which is visible from Brookdale Road, the main access to the arboretum. (Courtesy of Bartlett Arboretum & Gardens.)

Lower Back Cover (from left to right): The majestic redbud planted by Francis Bartlett is spectacular in spring flower. (Courtesy of Bartlett Arboretum & Gardens.) The stunning bark of the Korean stewartia offers year-round appeal. (Courtesy of Dan Lenore.) The greenhouse in winter beckons visitors to a welcome respite from the cold. (Courtesy of Hannah Heyman.)

Images of Modern America

BARTLETT ARBORETUM & GARDENS

S. Jane von Trapp and Bartlett Arboretum & Gardens
Foreword by Alice B. Smith and Hilary B. Forsyth

ARCADIA
PUBLISHING

ISBN 978-1-4671-2501-7

Published by Arcadia Publishing
Charleston, South Carolina

Printed in the United States of America

Library of Congress Control Number: 2016953993

For all general information, please contact Arcadia Publishing:
Telephone 843-853-2070
Fax 843-853-0044
E-mail sales@arcadiapublishing.com
For customer service and orders:
Toll-Free 1-888-313-2665

Visit us on the Internet at www.arcadiapublishing.com

To the hundreds of volunteers who have embodied the heart, the hand, and the soul of the arboretum.

Contents

Foreword

Taking a few moments to enjoy the peaceful surroundings at the Bartlett is one of life's pleasures. There is something about the serene atmosphere created by the lovely old trees that stand sentinel over the gardens that brings your senses back in tune with the day. Yet even in these quiet times, the Bartlett is alive with memories of past events that we have been involved with and of the people we have met along the way.

A glance at the greenhouse sitting quietly above the great lawn evokes just such a memory. Many a cold, snowy February we would celebrate a weekend of "Winter Bloom" when the greenhouse was filled with pots of flowering spring bulbs. In the autumn, our volunteer corps would pot up hundreds of tulip, daffodil, and narcissus bulbs. These were taken to the springhouse storage cellar over in the Conifer Garden, where they were stored for six weeks in the dark to force the bulbs into early growth. The pots were then transported back to the greenhouse, where they were cleaned up, watered, and nurtured into bloom in preparation for the big event. What a sight when Winter Bloom was set up and ready for customers! The greenhouse was transformed into a veritable paradise of blossom and fragrance, like a jewel glistening amidst the snow blanketing the fields. The beauty of it all quickly dispelled any memories of the hours of work involved, the freezing trips to and from the Conifer Garden cellar, the worrying over whether the bulbs would rot or fail to bloom on time. Why would we want to get involved in all of this hard work? Besides getting to enjoy the spectacular end result, it was the fun we had working with our fellow volunteers and the wonderful camaraderie of being with a group of like-minded people.

Winter Bloom is but one of the many projects that we have worked on over the years. These projects—gardens, plant sales, tours, gala events—are milestones in the history of the arboretum. In a way, our story has been woven into the fabric of the Bartlett Arboretum, along with the stories of the many people who have walked the same paths.

We feel so privileged to have been a part of it all.

—Alice B. Smith and Hilary B. Forsyth
Bartlett Arboretum Volunteers

ACKNOWLEDGMENTS

While only a few individuals are highlighted in this book, hundreds of volunteers have toiled at the arboretum over the years. It is impossible to name all who left their mark, but we are indebted to them. Our volunteers have collectively donated thousands of hours to keep the gardens colorful, weed-free, watered, pruned, and mapped, and to ensure their financial support. They also act as docents, greeters, committee and board members, event workers, and advisors. The arboretum has always been dependent on volunteers to keep it beautiful and functional.

The Arboretum Committee of 1964 was instrumental in turning a research lab into a public arboretum. We list each member's name here to acknowledge that without their efforts (together with the support of many elected officials), the property would not have been preserved: vice chairmen Malcolm J. Edgerton Jr., Henry C. Niewenhous, and Bradley A. Walker; art director Jack E. Brown; Mrs. James E. Hubbell—garden clubs; and area chairpeople Mrs. Frederick F. Robinson (Danbury), John Oldrin (Darien), Mrs. Alice Orme Smith (Fairfield-Bridgeport), Joseph A. Dietrich (Greenwich), Mrs. John D. Britton, (Hartford), Gordon Loery (Litchfield), Henry A. Caesar II (New Canaan), Kimberly Cheney (New Haven), Thaddeus G. Cowell Jr. (Westport-Weston), Mrs. Chester W. Kitchings (New London), Roy Wilcox (Meriden), Mr. and Mrs. Daniel M. McKeon (Ridgefield), Mrs. Jonathan Lanman (Stamford), Mrs. Rea King McCarty (Torrington), and Edmund K. Swigart (Washington).

Our membership grows each year, and we thank you for supporting the arboretum through good times and challenging ones. Cheers to Jonathan Arnow, Richard Burkhardt, Hilary Forsyth, Marion Glowka, Mark Greenwald, Peter Lyons, Nicholas Pettit, Gary Pitcock, Sally Sacks, and Alice Smith for sharing their memories. Thank you to our fact checkers, Patrick Franklin, Carol Levine, and Paul Travaglino.

We thank all the boards of directors of the Bartlett Arboretum Association Inc. that have served over the years for their unselfish and dedicated service to the arboretum. We thank the current board, chaired by Polly O'Brien Morrow, for its support of this project and for its steadfast commitment to preserving the property for future generations to enjoy. Polly Morrow also must be thanked for reading and editing this book before submission.

We thank the Bartlett family and Paul Dilworth and Patrick Franklin at the Bartlett Tree Research Laboratories in Charlotte, North Carolina, for opening up their archives to us.

Many thanks to Dan Lenore and the other photographers who donated their time and artistic talents toward making this book so beautiful. And we thank all of the unidentified photographers who captured the essence of the arboretum in images that have found their way into this book.

Finally, huge kudos go to Jane Alpert for tirelessly combing through hundreds of images and newsletters. Her dedication to the book's success leaves a true legacy for future generations who discover the arboretum.

Unless otherwise noted, all images appear courtesy of Bartlett Arboretum & Gardens.

INTRODUCTION

The Bartlett Arboretum & Gardens is a natural preserve like no other in southwestern New England. The property features 93 acres of open space—magnificent award-winning champion and notable trees, charming gardens, wildflower meadows, red maple wetlands and boardwalks, woodland walking trails, wildlife, and native habitats. For weekend gardeners to budding botanists, the arboretum offers a place to relax, learn, and unplug. It is one of the only public arboreta in Connecticut and is open 365 days a year. But its history begins decades before 1966.

The arboretum's namesake, Francis A. Bartlett, acquired a 30-acre farm in 1913 and lived and worked on the property until his death in 1963. Bartlett was attracted to the property for its orchards and large collection of native trees, and over the years, he assembled a number of woody plant specimens on the property from all over the world. Before the acquisition of the farm, he founded The F.A. Bartlett Tree Expert Company, and this site would become the perfect setting for the research and experimentation he envisioned for his future endeavors. Bartlett had grown up on a working farm and studied horticulture at the Massachusetts Agricultural College, now the University of Massachusetts, Amherst. Upon graduation, he taught horticulture at Hampton Normal and Agricultural Institute in Virginia, a school for former slaves now known as Hampton University. When he turned his attention to commercial ventures and started the company in 1907, Bartlett was struck by the lack of application of scientific methods in tree care. To remedy this, he dedicated the rest of his life to achieving better care of trees through research and scientific study, a principle that would become known in his company as "The Bartlett Way." He started the Bartlett School of Tree Surgery on the grounds in 1923 and the Bartlett Tree Research Laboratories in 1927. He added acreage and collections and created the foundation for the present-day arboretum. Bartlett's work would gain him a reputation as one of the founders of modern-day arboriculture (dendrology). The arboretum's beginnings are rooted in the work of Francis A. Bartlett.

In 1963, following Bartlett's death, The F.A. Bartlett Tree Expert Company was forced to sell the property in Stamford and began to move its research efforts, and some of its commercial operations, to North Carolina. Without a grassroots community preservation effort, the rare plantings and native forest areas of the property would have been lost to development. In 1964, a group of individuals came together to raise funds to purchase and preserve 64 acres of the property as a public arboretum to be utilized for botanical research, horticultural education, and community enjoyment of the natural environment. The group became known as the Arboretum Committee. Booth Hemingway, a Stamford resident and member of the Stamford Board of Representatives, was named chairman. The Arboretum Committee included members from all across Connecticut. This group raised more than $100,000 from private donations and the City of Stamford. It also negotiated with the State of Connecticut and the federal government to obtain an additional $400,000 in open space preservation funds. The Bartlett family also generously agreed to reduce the purchase price in support of the preservation initiative. The purchase was completed in November 1965 and ushered in an era of joint oversight between the University of Connecticut and the newly formed Bartlett Arboretum Association Inc. The latter organization was the not-for-profit organization that succeeded the Arboretum Committee.

There has been a lot of change at the arboretum since the property was purchased by Francis Bartlett. However, the mission has been constant: To provide education about botanical environments and the importance of preserving them for future generations. Today, in addition to some 80-plus acres of natural forested areas, the Bartlett Arboretum & Gardens is home to 11 display gardens and eight additional plant collections. Though many of the magnificent trees and the beginnings of most of the collections can be traced to the efforts of Dr. Bartlett, the display gardens arose during the period of collaboration with the University of Connecticut. Later, when the arboretum was transferred to the City of Stamford, there was increased focus on native plantings and the removal of nonnative, invasive species.

Walking the paths and trails of the arboretum while observing the gardens, collections, and native plantings is like walking down memory lane, each area and planting a reminder of the efforts of those who have toiled before. With maps and photographs from the archives, it is possible to locate the remnants of former gardens or collections, like the Yellow and Purple Gardens of the early Bartlett property. Land that had burgeoned from 30 acres to 200 was reduced to 64 acres, and much of Dr. Bartlett's experimental open areas became housing developments when the transfer to the University of Connecticut occurred. Buildings were removed and constructed, displacing collections. Though the exact acreage and composition of the gardens and collections may have changed, one thing is certain: Today's gardens and collections and the efforts of the gardeners and horticulturists that maintain them form the foundation of the future, just as the past efforts of Bartlett and all the others have formed the foundation for the present.

In 2002, the State of Connecticut transferred the title of the arboretum to the City of Stamford. Mayor Dannel Malloy put his trust in the non-profit Bartlett Arboretum Association, established in 1965, to assume operational control as managers of the property and programs, and a long-term lease was signed. A $2 million state grant-in-aid for building construction, renovations, and garden rehabilitation was awarded, and the arboretum was named Bartlett Arboretum & Gardens. Twenty-seven more acres were added, resulting in a total of 91 acres of woodlands and open space, including the legacy plant collections established by Francis A. Bartlett and University of Connecticut professors and students. The Bartlett Arboretum & Gardens was now responsible for maintaining the acreage and remaining buildings and for creating an engaging public space for Stamford and the region. In 2014, facilitated by arboretum neighbor and former board chair Peter Lyons, two acres contiguous to the one-acre Conifer Garden were gifted to the association by Ann Baur, laying the groundwork for establishing a conifer reference garden and extending the acreage to 93.

In an effort to increase membership and support and promote its mission, the arboretum has invested in several programs and events over the years. Highlighted in this book are some of the outstanding examples of the staff- and volunteer-driven events conducted during more than 50 years of the arboretum's history. Some have survived and thrived, while others have evolved or been phased out.

One

Our Roots

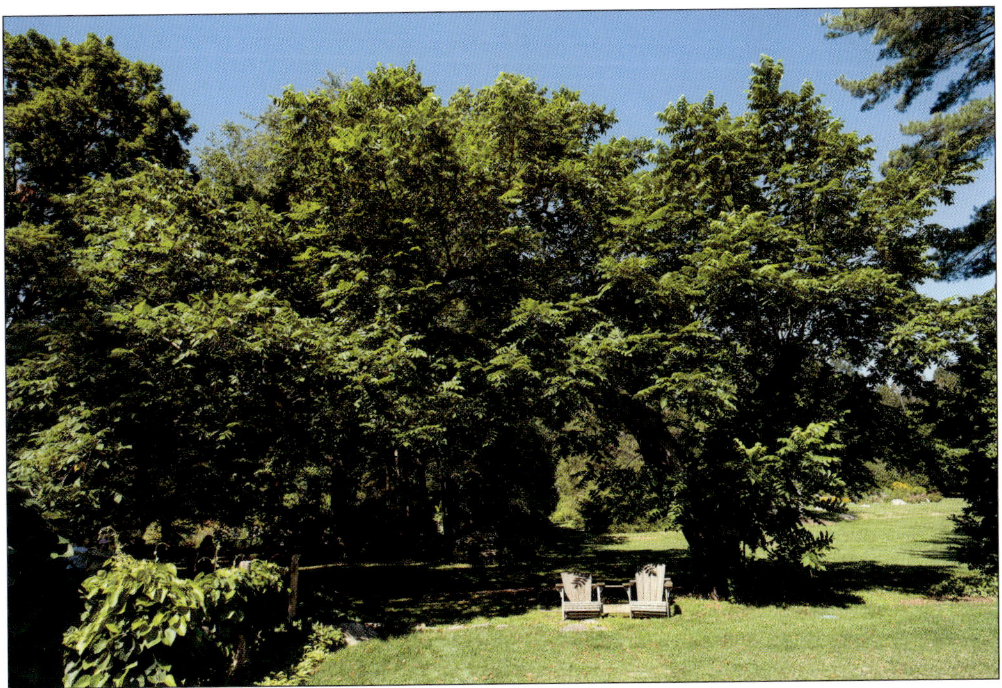

The Heart of the Arboretum. This history is rooted in the vision of the "father of arboriculture," Francis Bartlett. Of the many trees he planted on the property, none are more majestic than the heartnut, which he could see from his bedroom window. Its beamy silhouette presides over the heart of the arboretum today as a bridge to the past, giving hope for the future. (Courtesy of Dan Lenore.)

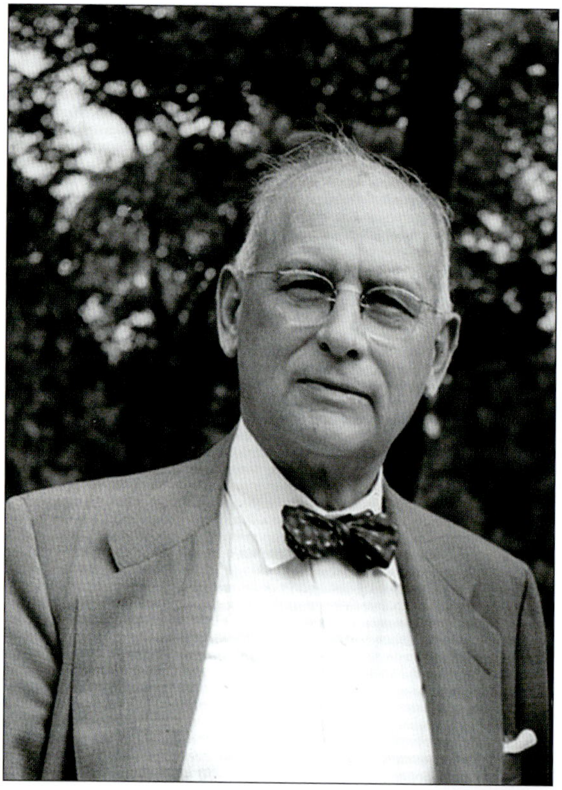

Dr. F.A. Bartlett. According to *The Bartlett Way*, Francis Alonzo Bartlett was born in November 1882 on a farm in Belchertown, Massachusetts. He studied botany and horticulture under the tutelage of Dr. George E. Stone at the Massachusetts Agricultural College, today the University of Massachusetts, Amherst. Upon graduation in 1905, he took his first job at the Hampton Normal and Agricultural Institute (now Hampton University) in Virginia, an institution formed to educate former slaves and their descendants. At Hampton Normal, he taught horticulture and supervised the institute's nursery and orchards. While there, Dr. Bartlett began offering his services as a paid consultant in the area of tree care and propagation to various landowners. This would set him on the path of eventually leaving teaching and creating a business offering tree care services to individuals and government agencies. (Both, courtesy of The F.A. Bartlett Tree Expert Company.)

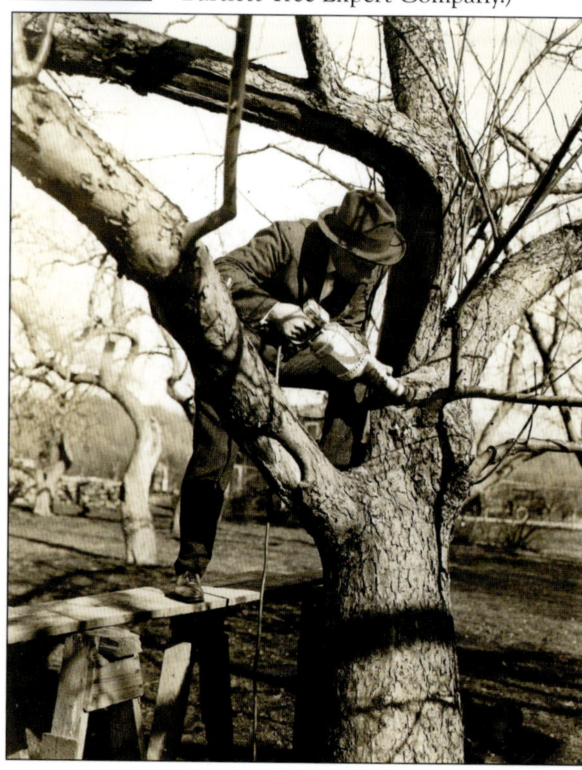

Move to the Northeast. In 1907, Dr. Bartlett left Hampton Normal to pursue business opportunities full time. He determined that the New York City area presented many potential business prospects. He relocated to White Plains, New York, and set up business with a college acquaintance, Harold L. Frost. The business focused on the provision of tree care to estate owners. Frost provided the financial backing, while Dr. Bartlett was in charge of sales and operations. This business was known as The Frost & Bartlett Company. By 1908, the business had clients in New York, Massachusetts, Pennsylvania, Connecticut, and New Jersey. Bartlett traveled to his customers by train. Dr. Bartlett finally relocated to Stamford, Connecticut, because it had better rail access to his customers. In 1909, he bought out Frost's interest in the business for a $5,000 personal note. (Both, courtesy of The F.A. Bartlett Tree Expert Company.)

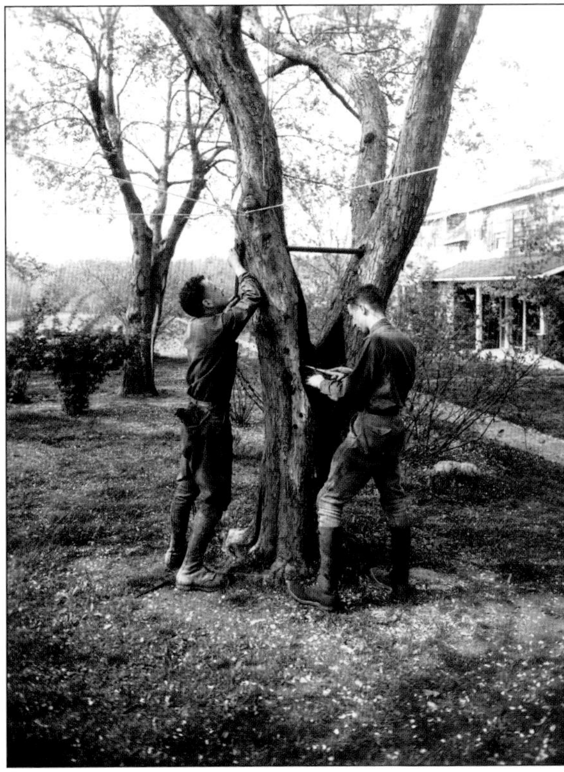

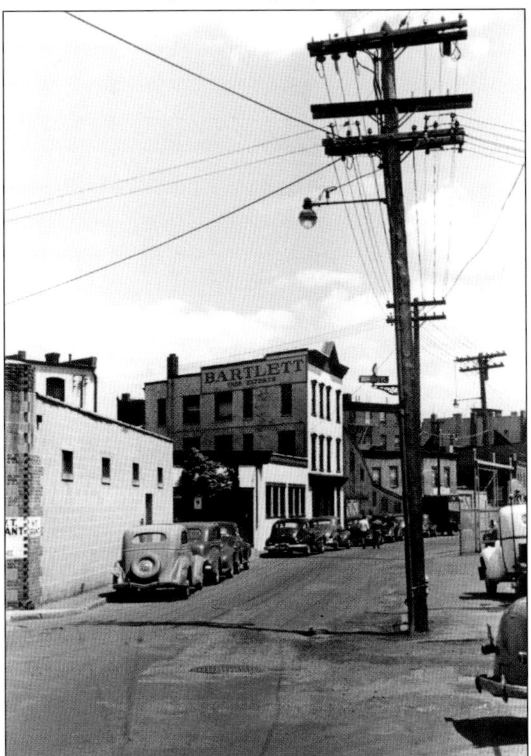

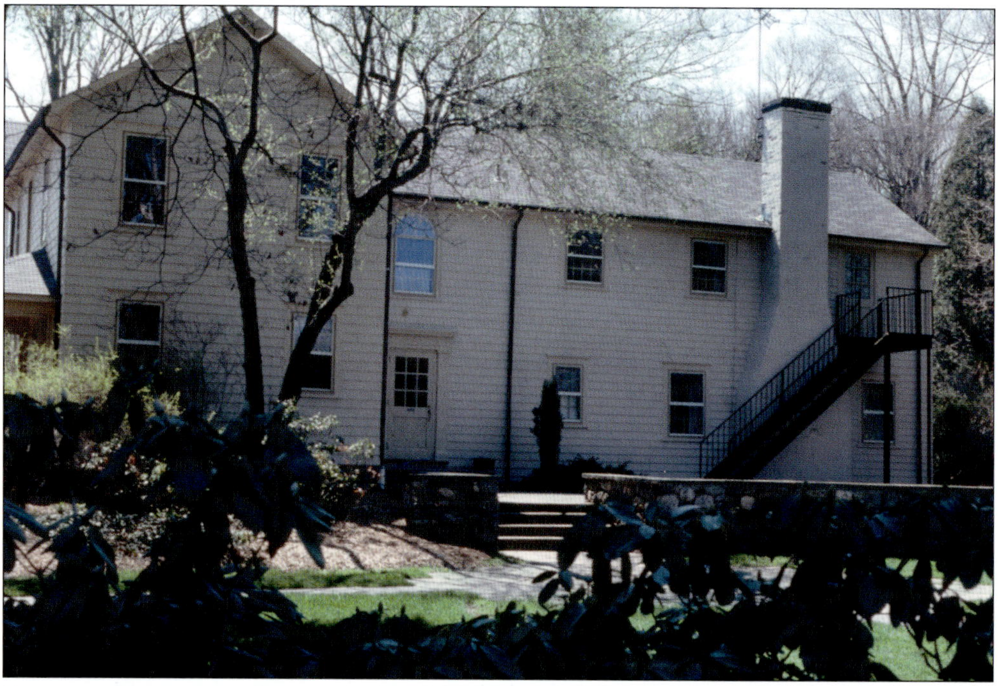

Bartlett Homestead, Rear and Side Views. In 1913, Dr. Bartlett bought a 30-acre farm in Stamford on Brookdale Road. The property had a farmhouse (today referred to as the "Homestead"), an orchard, and many hardwood trees. Everything to the left of the vertical downspout on the back view of the house (above), directly to the right of the entrance off the terrace, is part of the original structure. Dr. Bartlett moved to this house with his wife, Myrtle, shortly after their marriage. Their children, Robert (1917) and Jane (1922), were born here. The Homestead still stands today, serving as Bartlett Arboretum & Gardens's staff offices. In 2012, the house was remodeled, featuring hand-painted walls, elegant furnishings, and unique flourishes that harken back to its original construction.

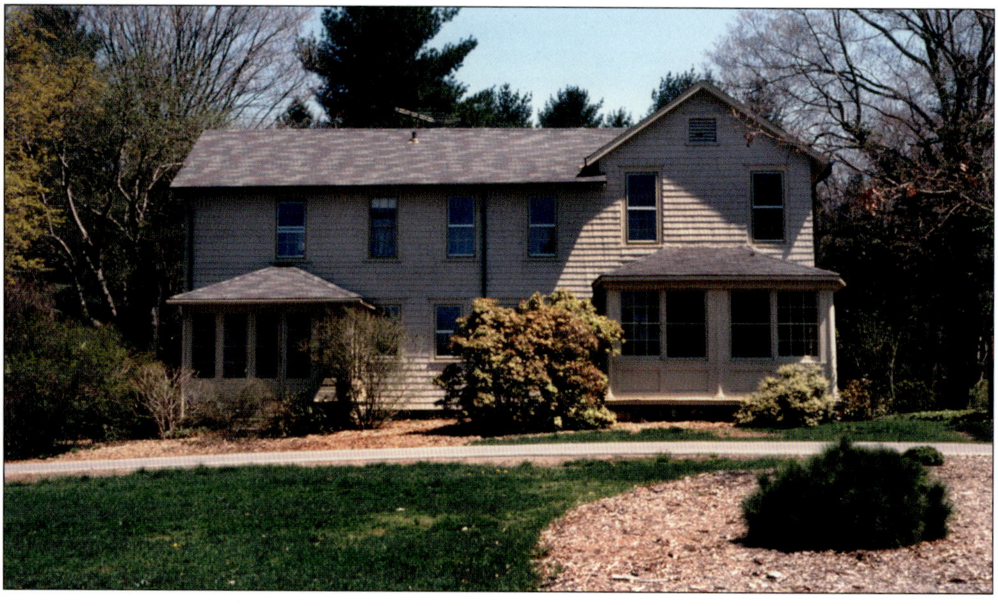

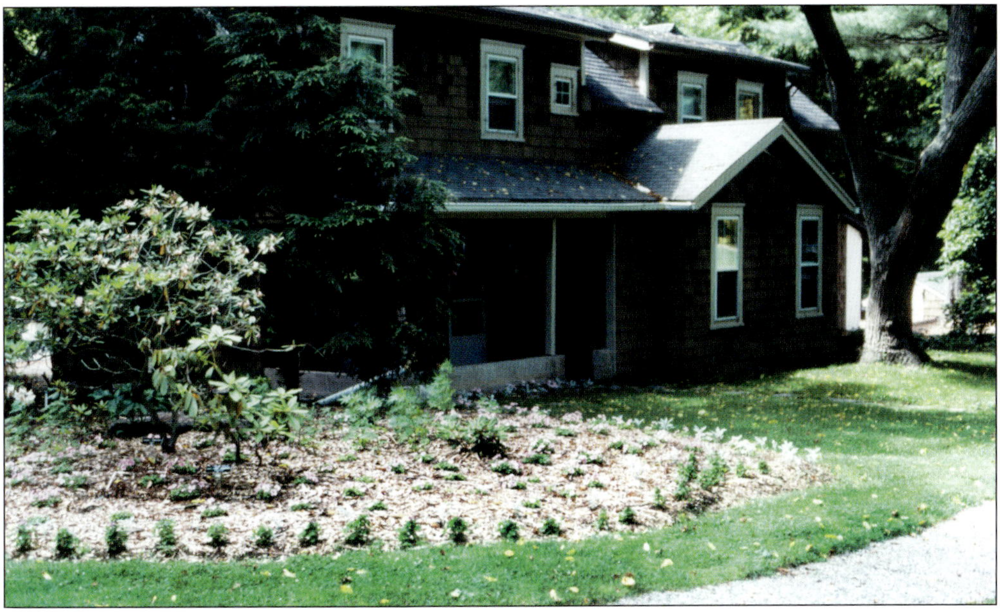

COTTAGE IN BACK OF HOMESTEAD. A small cottage was built behind the old house in 1934. It might originally have been a storage shed but was later used as living space for the arboretum caretaker and storage for equipment and tools. It also became the backdrop for an English cottage garden. It was destroyed by a fallen pine tree during Hurricane Sandy in 2012.

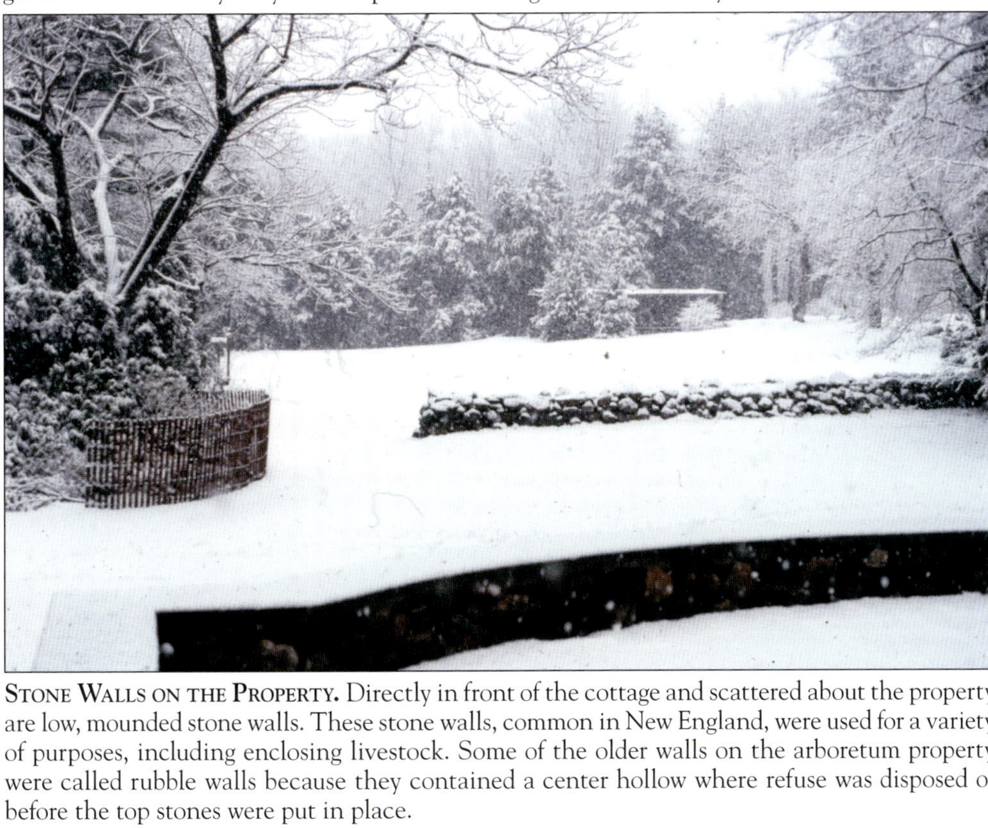

STONE WALLS ON THE PROPERTY. Directly in front of the cottage and scattered about the property are low, mounded stone walls. These stone walls, common in New England, were used for a variety of purposes, including enclosing livestock. Some of the older walls on the arboretum property were called rubble walls because they contained a center hollow where refuse was disposed of before the top stones were put in place.

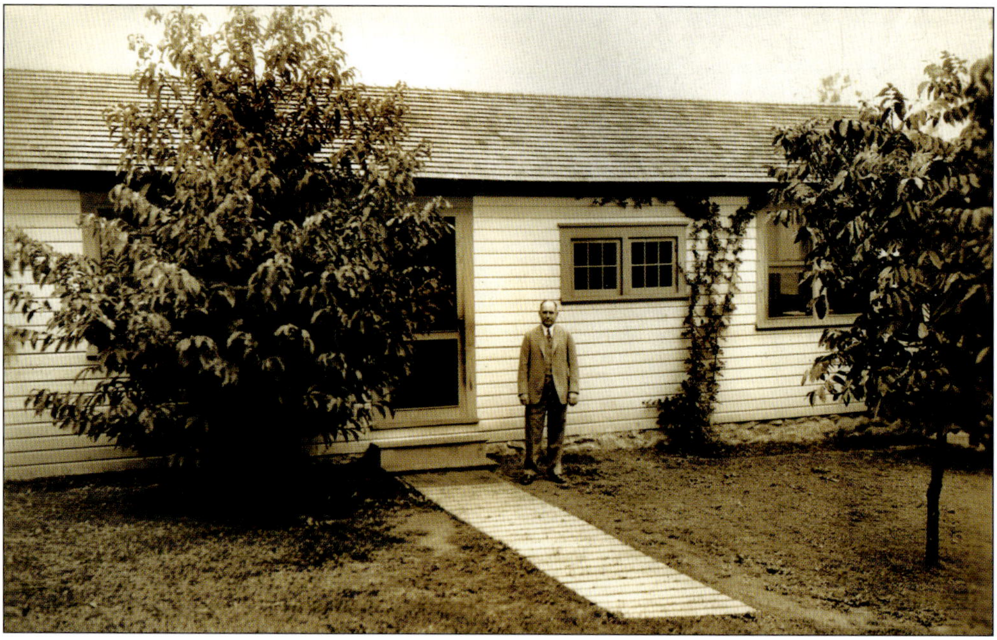

Stone Laboratory. In 1924, Dr. Bartlett decided he needed a formal laboratory to further his scientific work on tree care. He had a building constructed on the property and named it Stone Laboratory for his mentor and professor at Massachusetts Agricultural College, George E. Stone. The building itself was used for classroom work as well as plant pathology research. It was home to not only laboratories, but also culture and dark rooms to support the research activities. The above image shows F.A. Bartlett outside the Stone Laboratory. Below are Dr. E. Porter Felt (left), chief entomologist and first director of the Bartlett Tree Research Laboratories, and another scientist working inside. Dr. Felt joined Dr. Bartlett full time in 1927 but had been conducting research at the Bartlett property since 1915. (Both, courtesy of The F.A. Bartlett Tree Expert Company.)

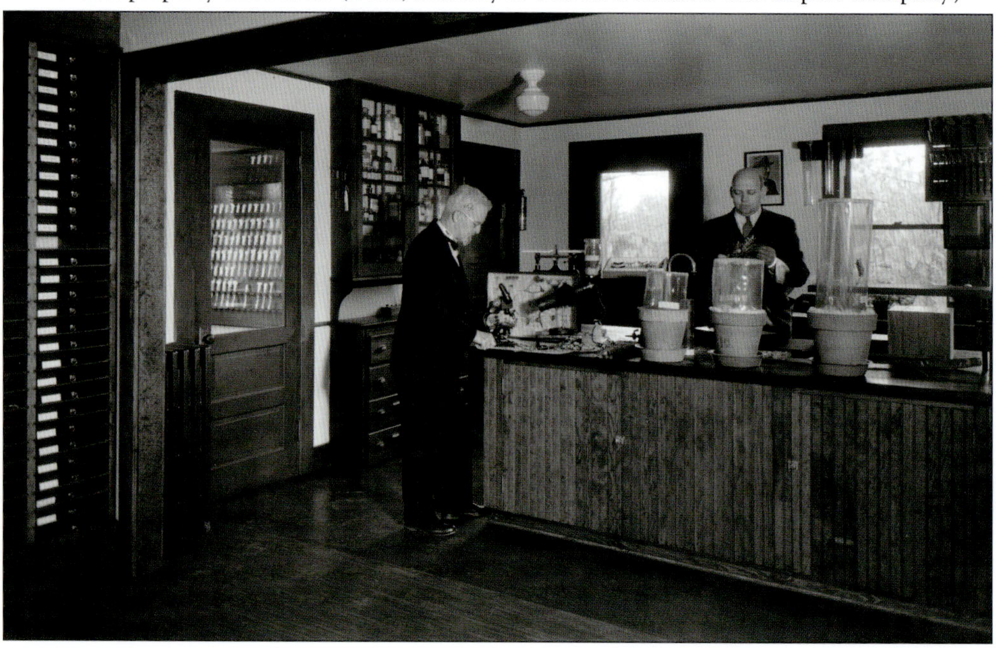

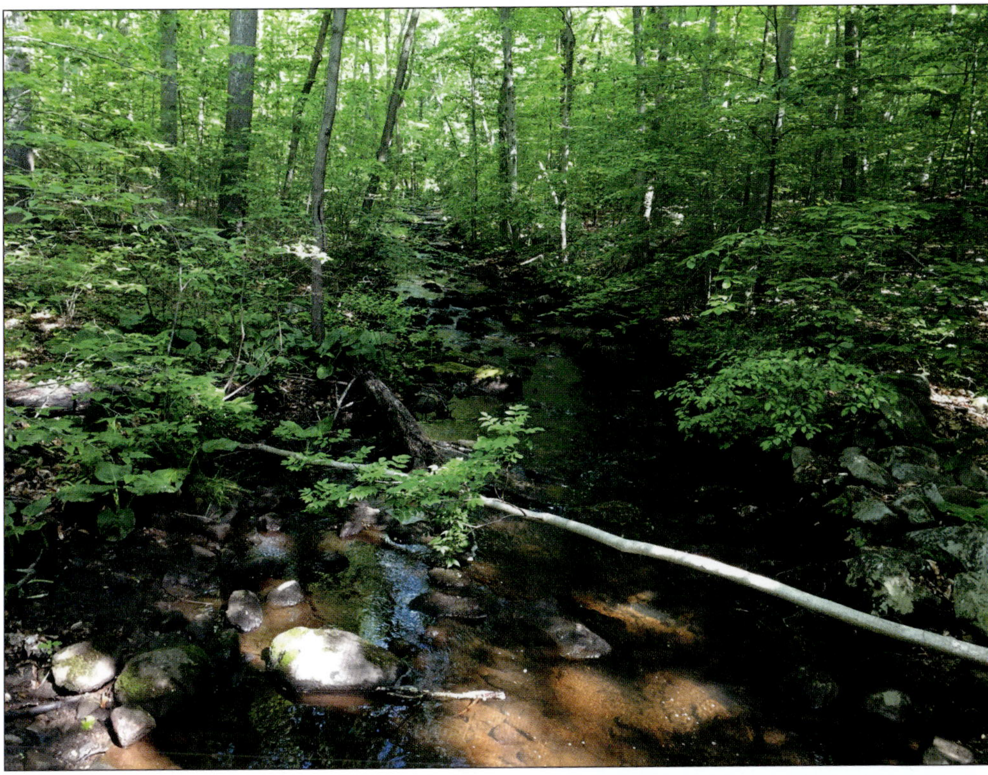

Poorhouse Brook. There are a brook and a pond on the grounds that supplied water for the property's operations during the early years. Poorhouse Brook, a fast-moving stream, acquired its name because it flows past the site of a former poorhouse, or farm for indigents. The foundation of the poorhouse can be found northwest of the parking lot near Potter's Field Cemetery.

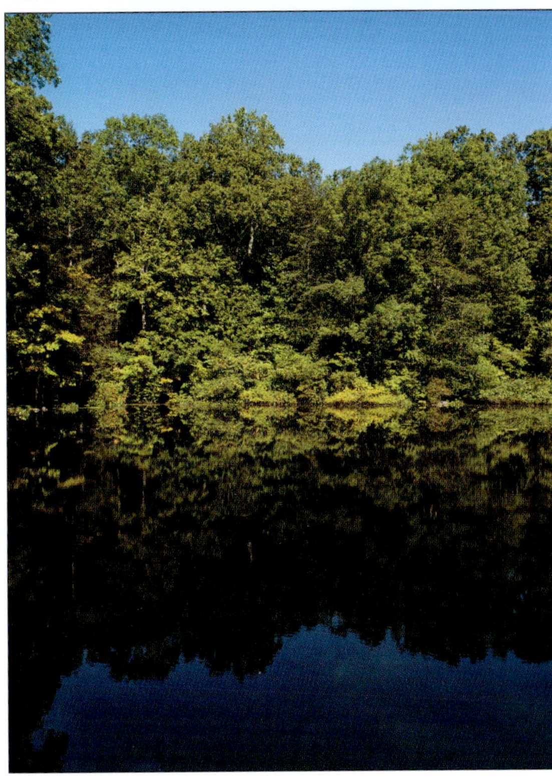

Forsyth Pond. The woodland pond was created by a dam located at the point where the water pauses before spilling into Poorhouse Brook. The water then runs south to Long Island Sound. Shallow enough for aquatic plants to root and still reach the surface, Forsyth Pond is home to frogs, dozens of snapping turtles, several aquatic plants, and cypress trees planted by Bartlett. (Courtesy of Dan Lenore.)

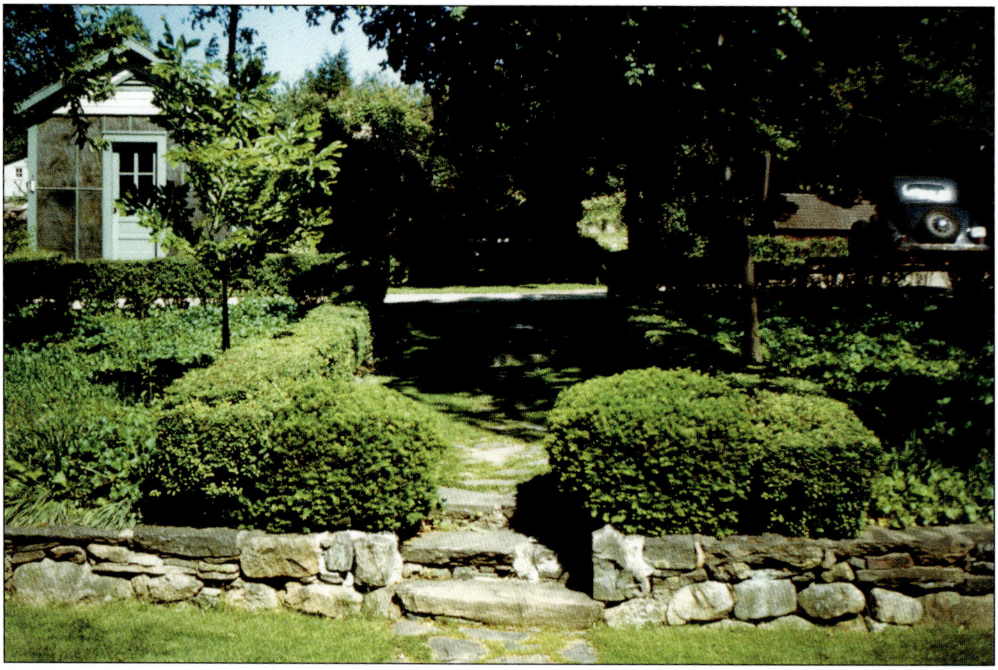

Insectary. Dr. Bartlett added an insectary in 1928 across the driveway from the Stone Laboratory. This building was screened so that outdoor temperatures could be maintained and experiments on the life cycle of insects in their actual climate could be conducted. Once Dr. Bartlett learned about the different stages of the insects and which stages were the most destructive to trees and plants, he was able to find the best solutions for control. Pictured are internal and external views of the insectary. The bagging over the plants inside served to contain a certain species of insect to one variety of plant. (Below, courtesy of The F.A. Bartlett Tree Expert Company.)

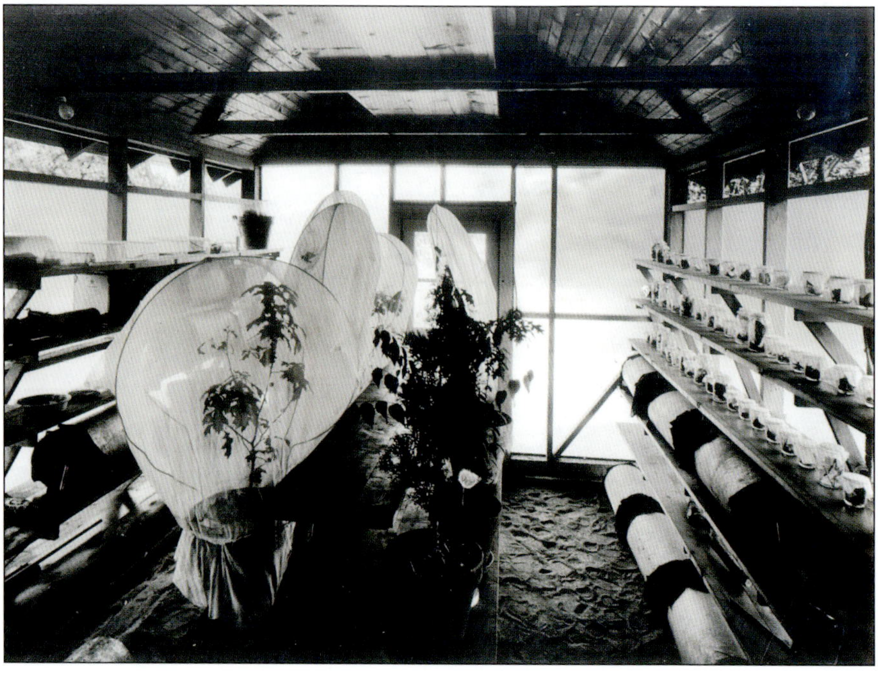

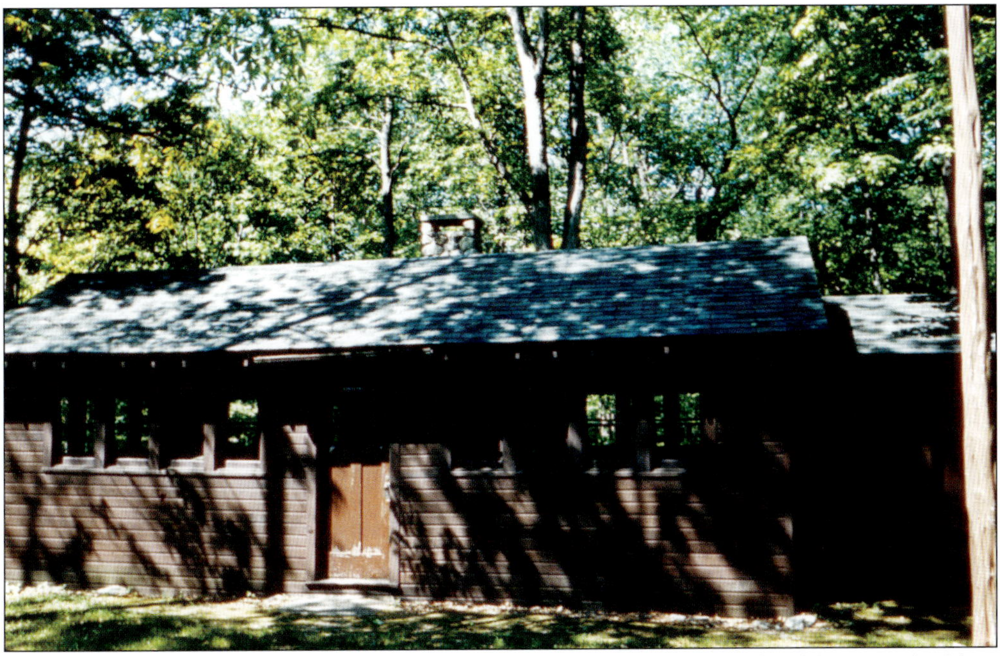

Forsyth Laboratory. As the school and scientific research grew, another laboratory building was constructed in 1929 on the lower part of the property adjacent to the pond, near the spillway. Dr. Bartlett named this laboratory for William Forsyth, a leading figure in the development of arboriculture. At the close of the 18th century, Forsyth developed a method for filling tree cavities using a recipe of "fresh cow dung, old lime, wood ashes, and sand," according to *Our Heritage of Community Trees*. Dr. Bartlett and his scientists experimented with other materials for filling tree cavities, including cement, a method no longer used today. The popular flowering shrub *Forsythia* (below) is named after Forsyth.

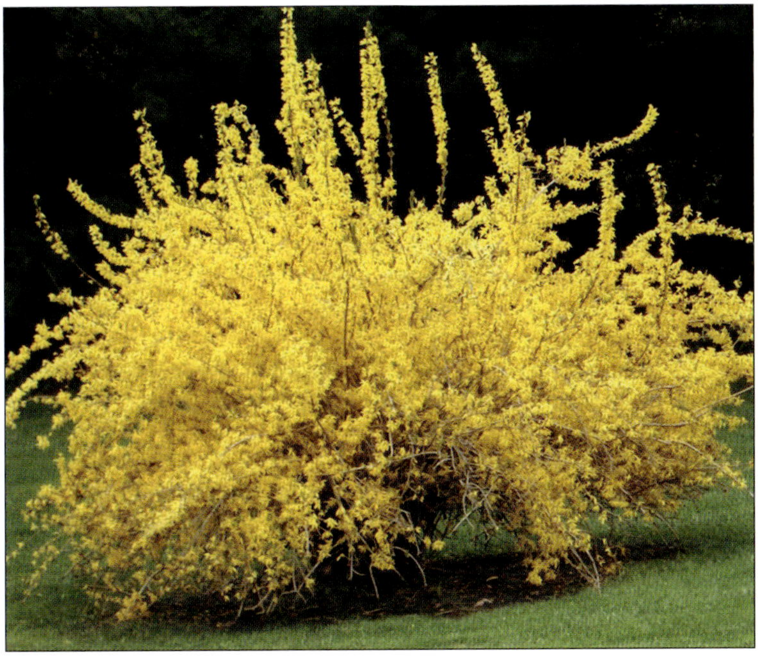

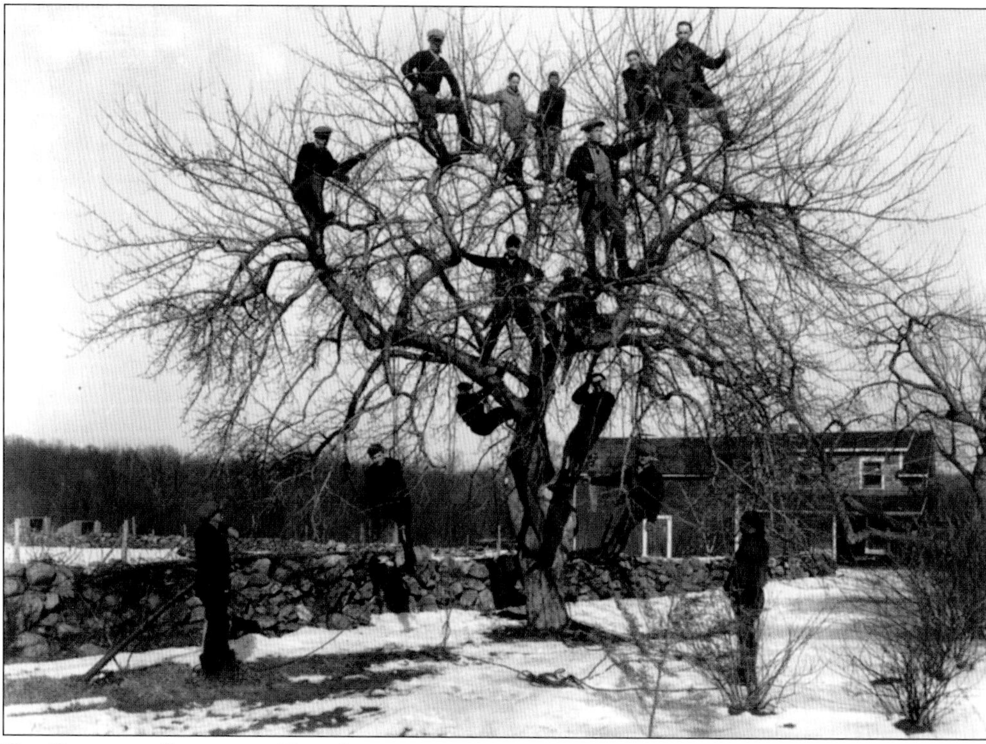

The Bartlett School of Tree Surgery. In 1923, Dr. Bartlett officially established the Bartlett School of Tree Surgery to train young men in horticulture and tree care, including knowledge of tree growth, tree sanitation, cavity treatment, pruning, bracing and cabling, prevention of girdling roots, lightning protection, and fertilizing. Bartlett and the staff at the school pioneered many innovative techniques and equipment for pruning and care of trees that are still used today. Above, the men in the tree are the first class of the school in 1924. Lem Strout, standing on the ground at left, was an instructor at the school. Pictured below is another class at Stone Laboratory. (Both, courtesy of The F.A. Bartlett Tree Expert Company.)

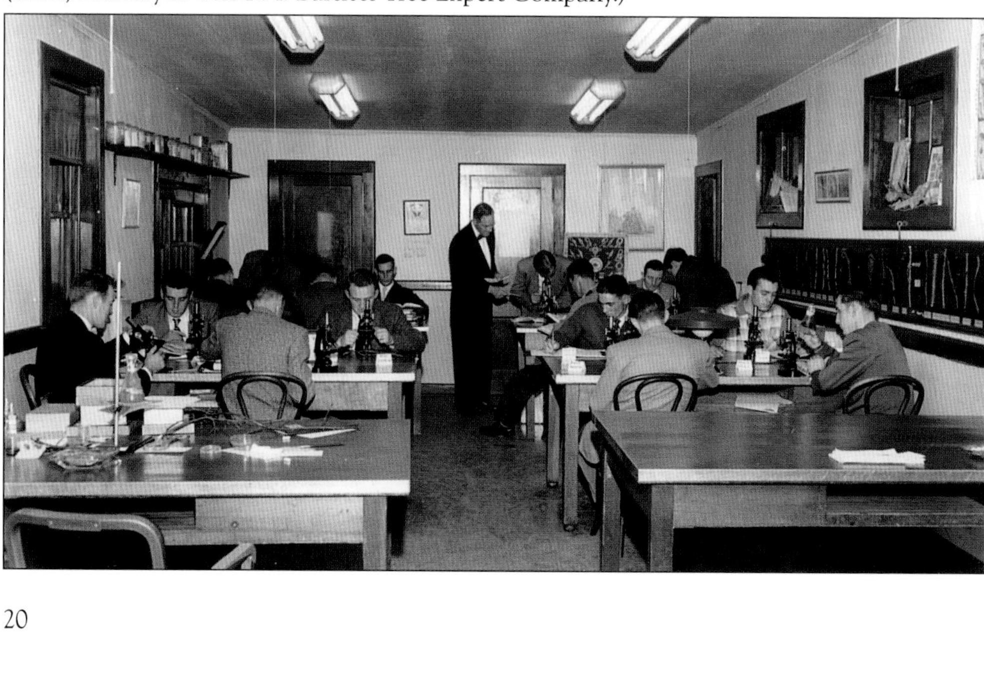

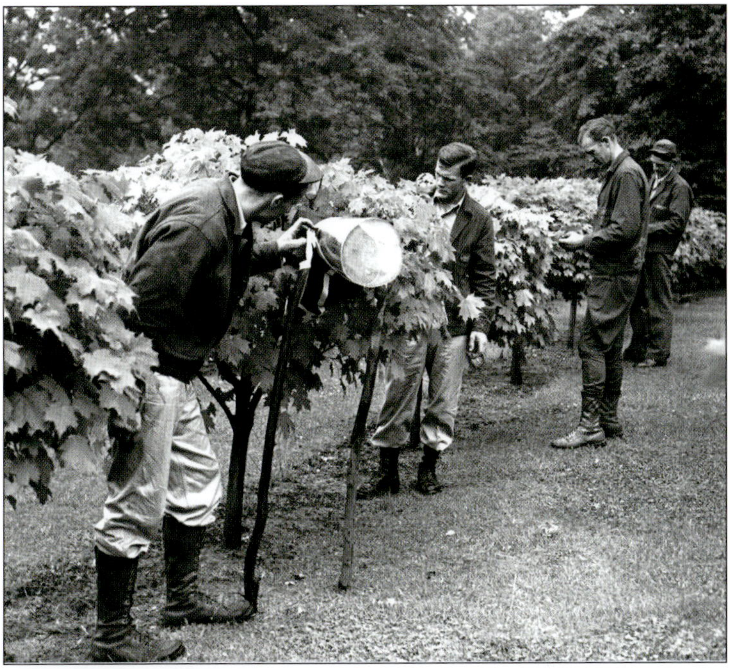

Learning Outside the Classroom. Students in the Bartlett School of Tree Surgery class of 1946 and other Bartlett crew members inspect a row of young sugar maples planted on the Bartlett grounds for the study of diseases and insects. The Bartlett School of Tree Surgery also reached out to veterans of World War II to offer them a lifelong vocation in arboriculture. (Courtesy of The F.A. Bartlett Tree Expert Company.)

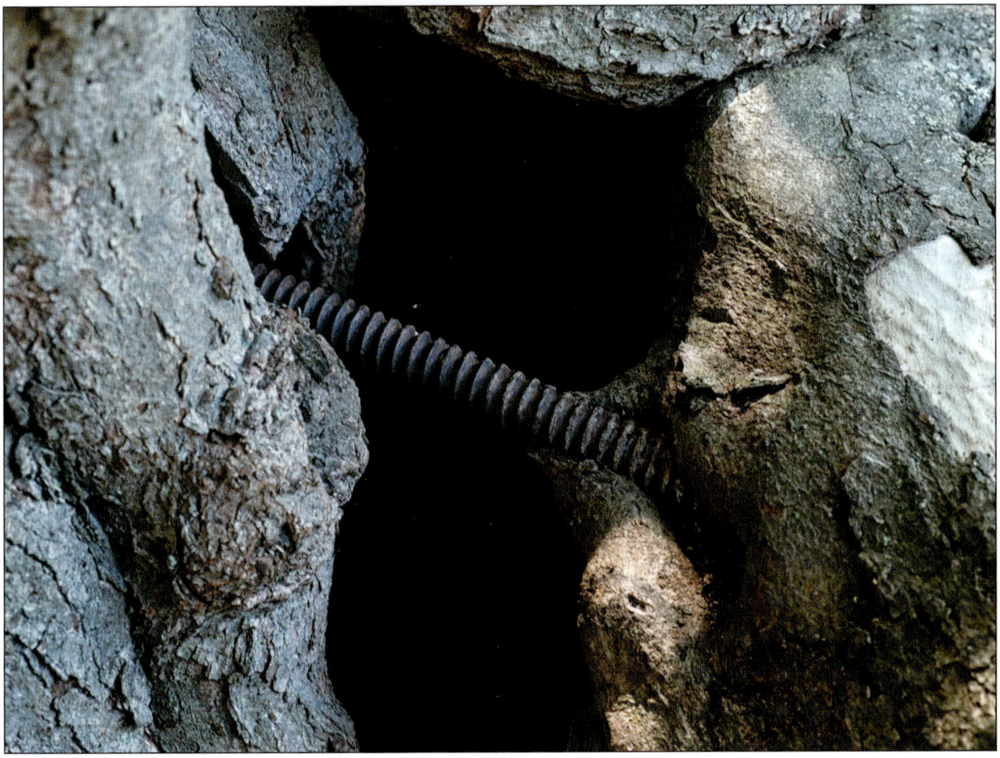

Bracing and Cabling Used Today. Examples of bracing and cabling that were taught at the Bartlett School of Tree Surgery can be seen on many of the older trees at the arboretum today. Pictured here is an example of bracing installed by The F.A. Bartlett Tree Expert Company on the aging redbud (*Cercis canadensis*) located on the arboretum grounds. (Courtesy of Dan Lenore.)

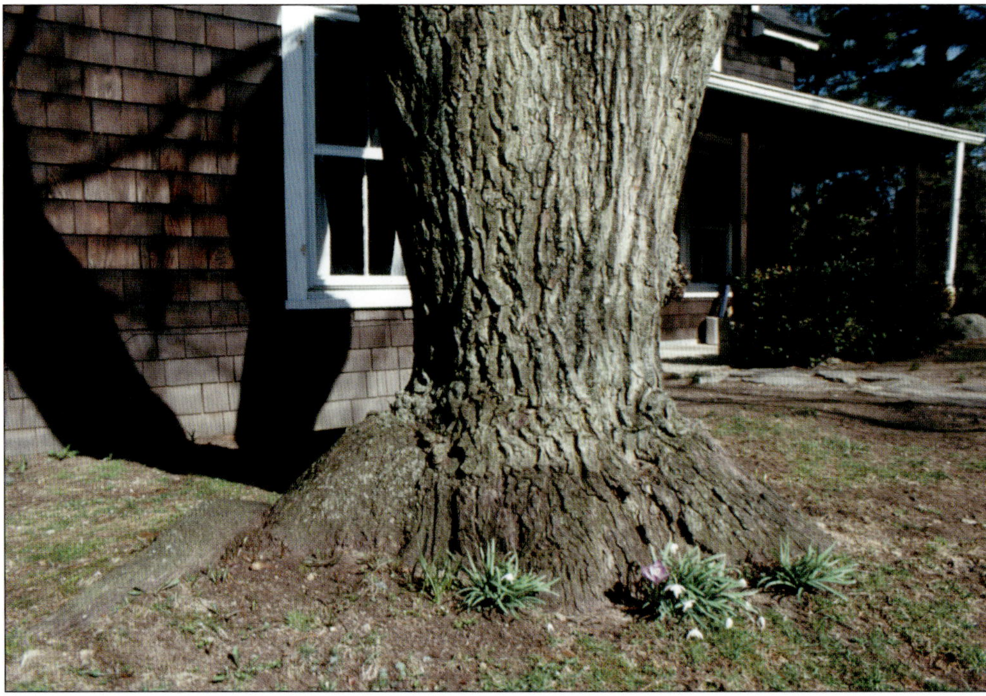

Grafting. Dr. Bartlett and the faculty and students of the Bartlett School of Tree Surgery also conducted experiments on grafting one species of tree onto the roots of another, a technique used to expedite growth and improve hardiness. One of the early experiments was the graft of the heartnut, also known as the Japanese walnut (*Juglans ailantifolia*), onto the roots of butternut (*Juglans cinerea*) stock. The heartnut is so called because it produces an edible, heart-shaped nut. Grafting techniques expedite growth of nut and fruit trees, permitting the trees to bear fruit sooner than they would without grafting. This can be a significant commercial benefit. The heartnut can be seen today beyond the Homestead terrace (below) with the graft line clearly visible.

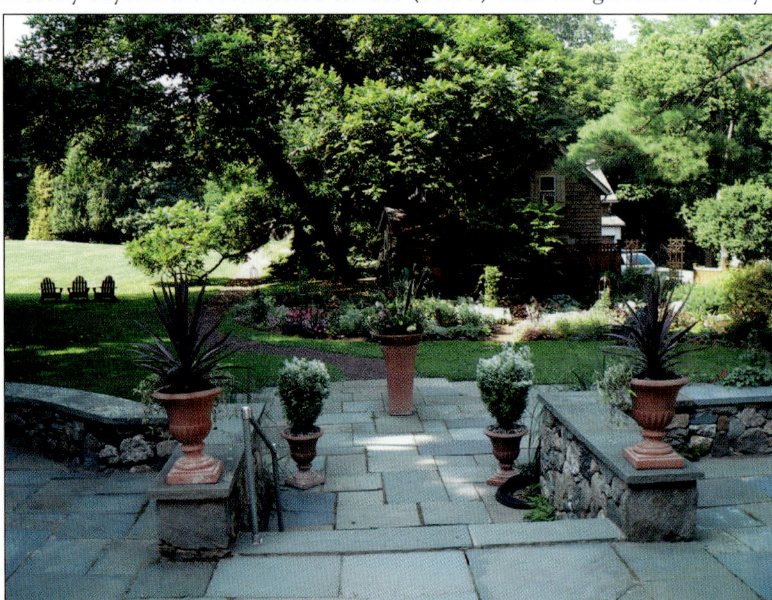

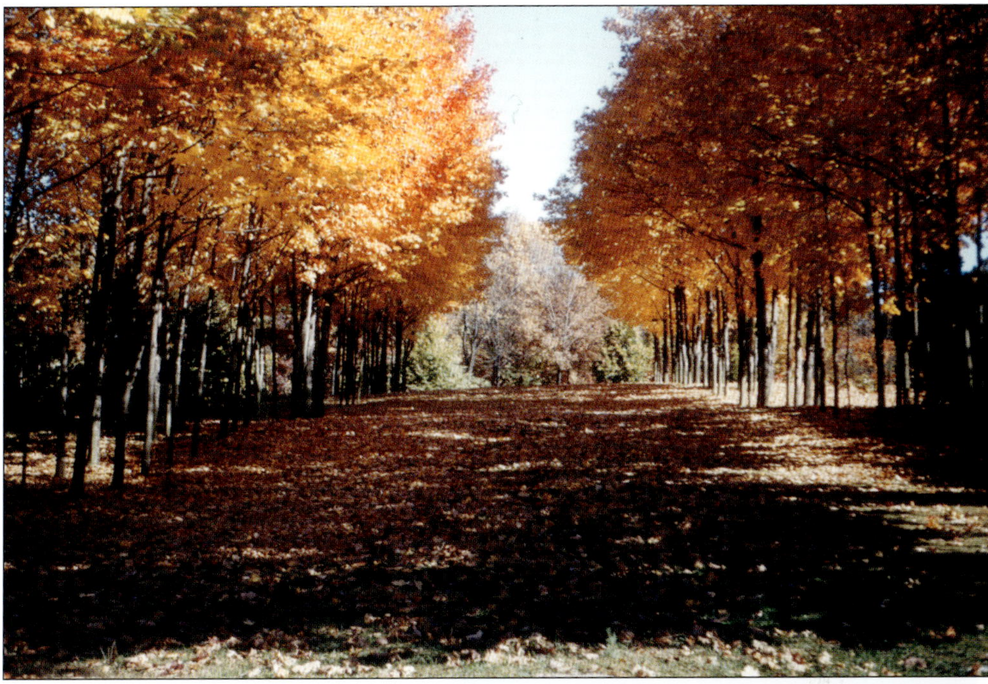

Experimenting with Landscape Forms. As Dr. Bartlett acquired more land, eventually increasing his holdings to about 200 acres, he was able to experiment with landscape designs. One such design was the creation of allées. An allée is a landscape technique in which a border is created along a road or path using the same type of tree or shrub to direct the viewer's vision to an end point, often the major building on the property. It was a design popular in Europe in the early 1900s and copied in the Americas. Another form was to create a hedge out of local, native trees and shrubs, pruned to uniform shape, known as a "poor man's hedge." Pictured here are two allées that Dr. Bartlett planted on the property: The sugar maple allée (*Acer saccharum*, above) and the arborvitae allée (*Thuja occidentalis*, right).

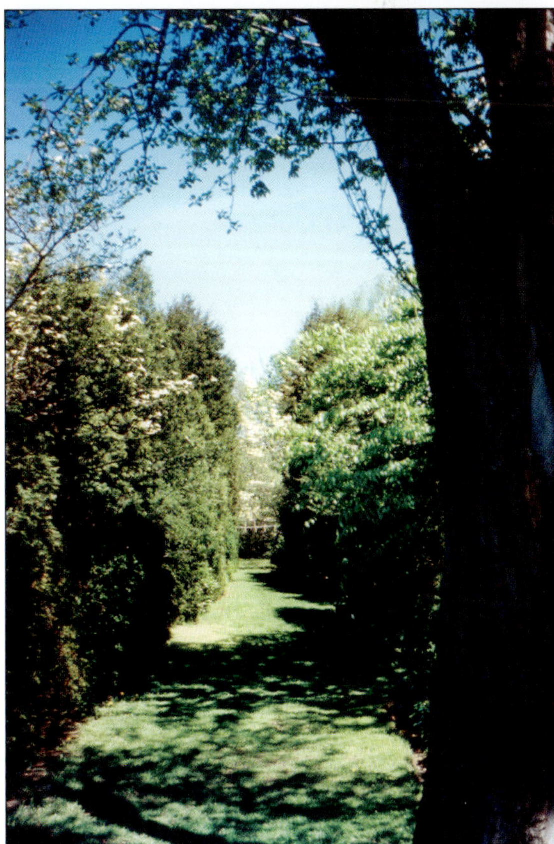

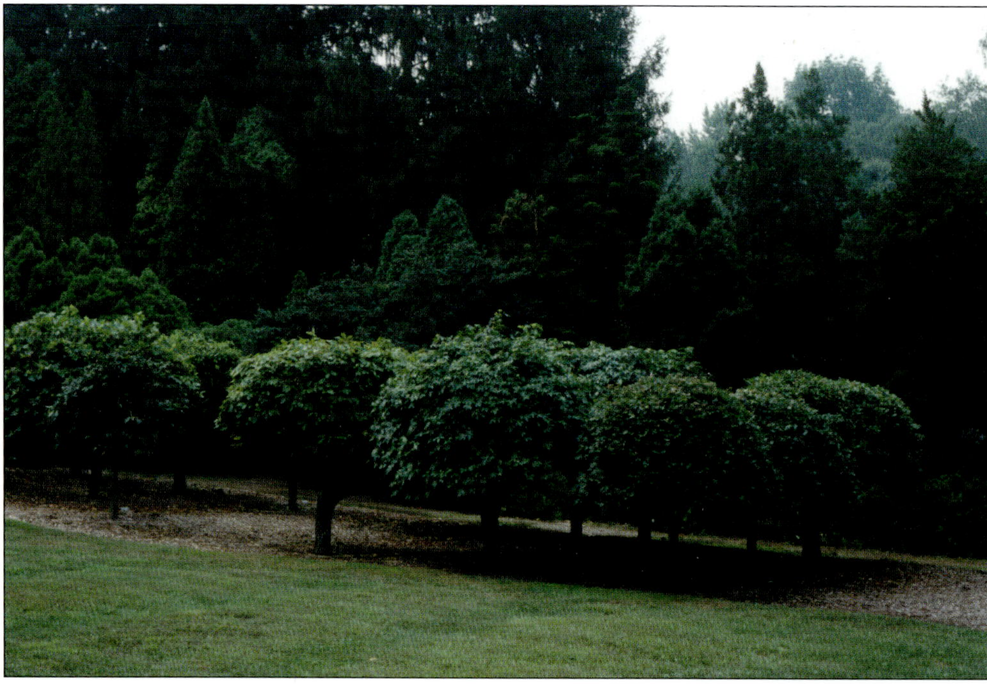

Pollarding Trees for Size and Form. Dr. Bartlett and his staff planted rows of trees that were pruned back to the same point each year, giving them a stunted, uniform look and stature, another popular early European style. Each year, measurements would be taken so that they could be consistently maintained to a precise height and width. This technique keeps the trees compact when space is limited. The visual impact of the uniform rows made pollarded tree gardens popular with some of Bartlett's customers. The tree gardens also served as living experiments. Bartlett scientists and students would introduce insects and diseases onto some of the trees and would compare and monitor the impact of the insects and diseases by comparison to neighboring trees of the exact size and shape. At the end of each season, the diseased material would be removed.

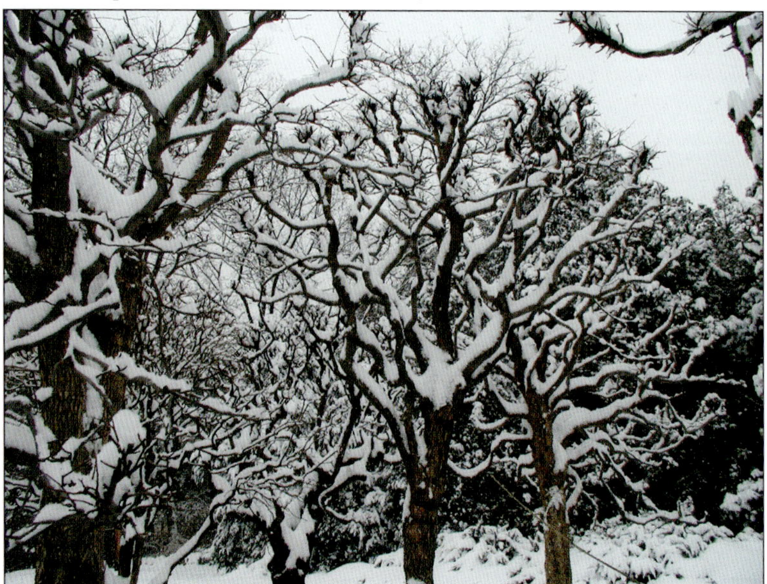

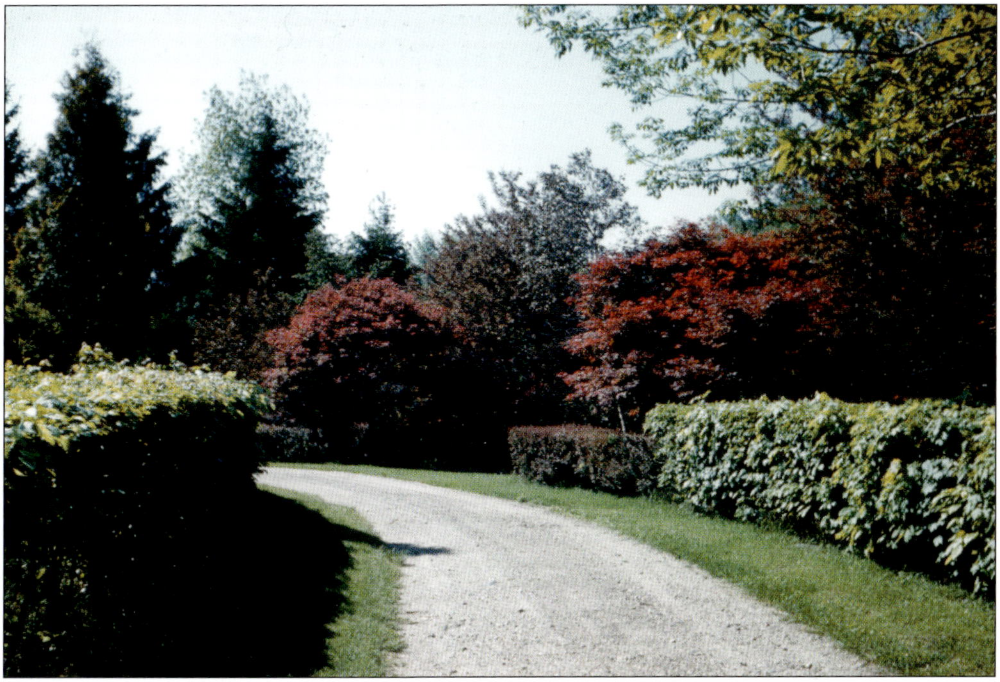

Color-Themed Gardens. Experiments were also done with color-themed gardens. Two of the most distinctive were the Purple Garden and the Golden or Yellow Garden. The Purple Garden was a collection of purple and reddish-leaved trees and shrubs. The hedge in the Purple Garden was composed of purple-leaved Japanese barberry (*Berberis thunbergii* var. *atropurpurea*). This was a U-shaped formal garden. Bordering the Purple Garden was the Golden or Yellow Garden. This garden was filled with yellow-leaved trees and shrubs that gave off a golden hue in the sunlight. Remnants of these gardens can be found today on the arboretum property.

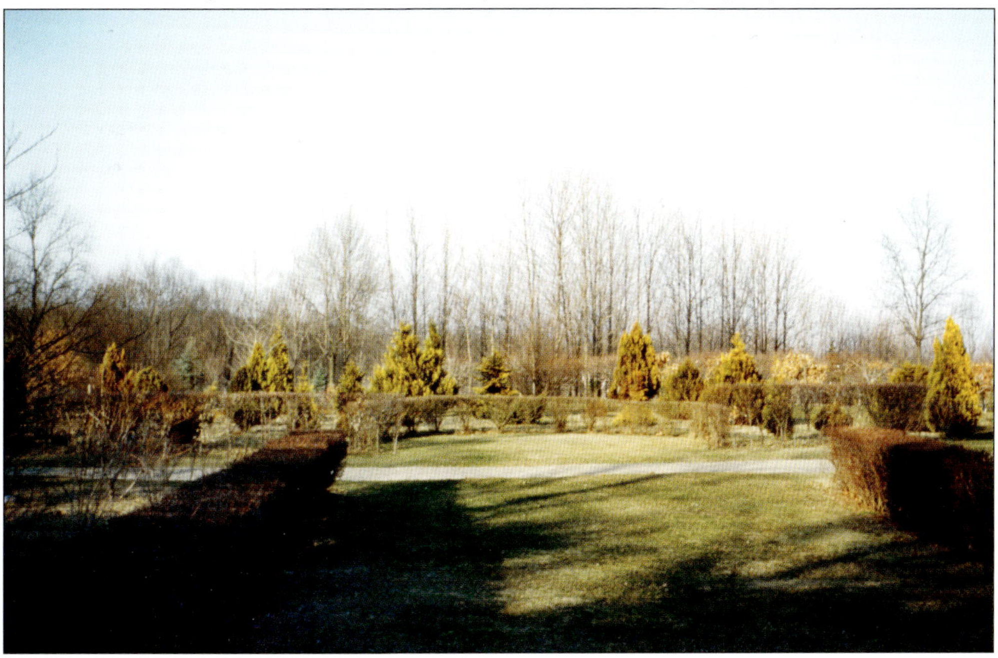

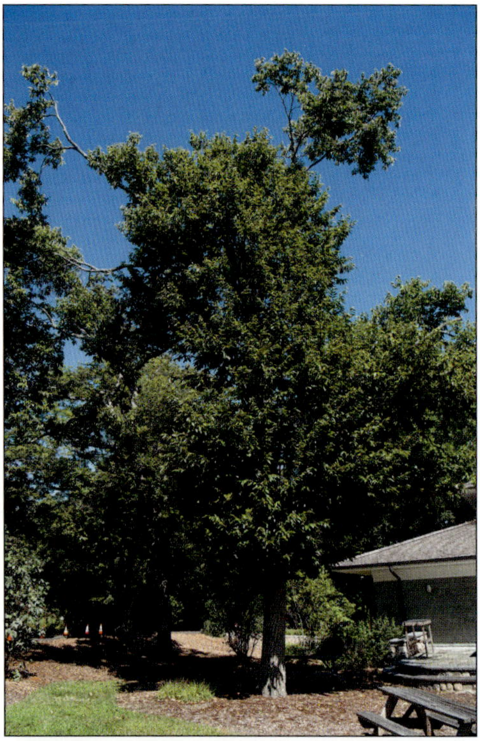

Bartlett Chestnut (*Castanea mollissima* x). The American chestnut (*C. dentata*) was an important commercial resource for the lumber industry in the United States until chestnut blight was introduced from Japan in 1904. Most of the native trees perished over the next 50 years. In 1916, the US Bureau of Plant Industry sent hybrid seedlings (Chinese chestnut crossed with an unknown hybrid) to experts across the country, including to Dr. Bartlett. Only Dr. Bartlett's seedling proved to be resistant to both disease and cold. In 1934, this tree was named the Bartlett Chestnut by the US Department of Agriculture. It grew with multiple stems rather than a single trunk, but the form and flavor of the nut is similar to the native American chestnut. Several offspring, such as these beauties, can be seen at the arboretum today. (Both, courtesy of Dan Lenore.)

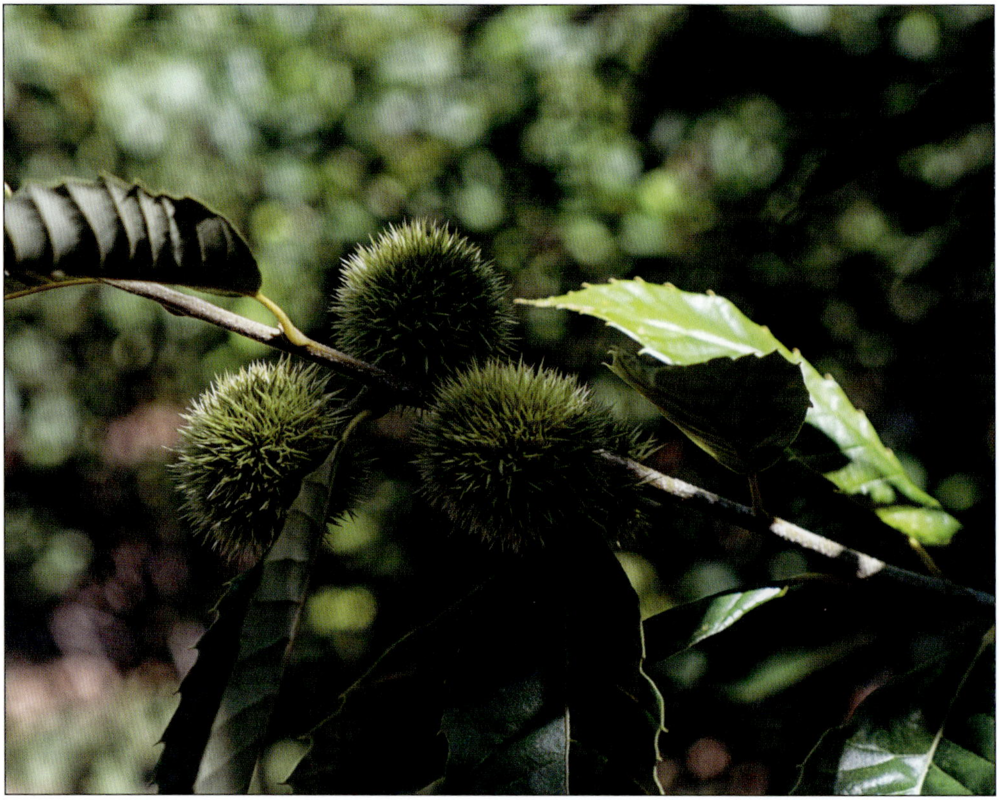

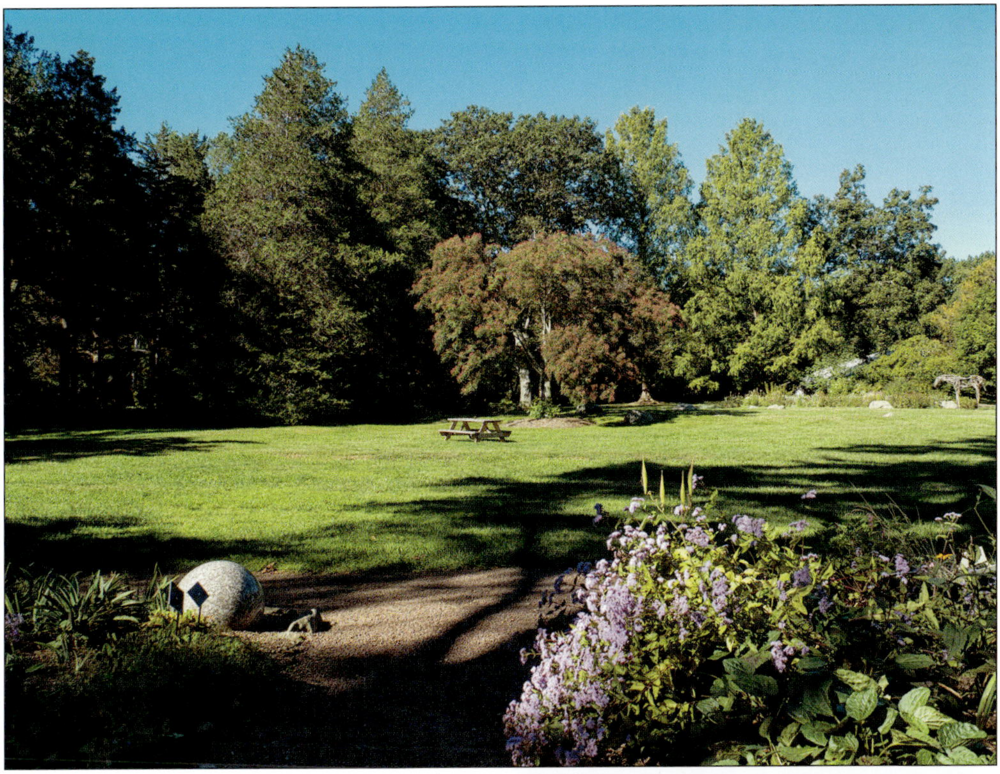

Exotic Trees. There are many trees on the property that were sent by scientists from other countries or acquired by Dr. Bartlett from far off places to determine whether they would be hardy in the New England climate and of use either for home landscaping or commercial purposes. The Korean evodia (above, in foreground) or bee bee tree (*Tetradium daniellii*), beloved by beekeepers for its small white flowers that are attractive to bees, thrives on the arboretum grounds. Another unusual tree, far from its native home in Chile, is the monkey puzzle tree (*Araucaria araucana*) pictured at right. A favorite for its evergreen, sharply pointed leaves on branches arranged in a spiral around the trunk, this tree proved to be poorly adapted to New England winters. The original specimen planted by Dr. Bartlett did not survive, but today the arboretum maintains a specimen in its greenhouse.

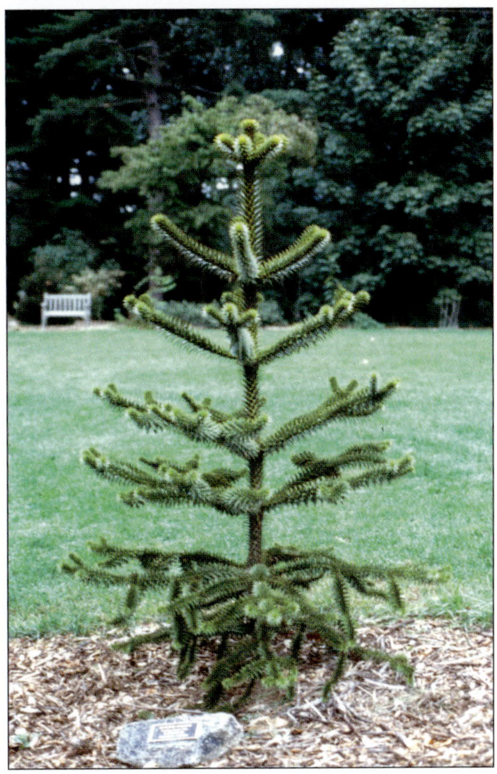

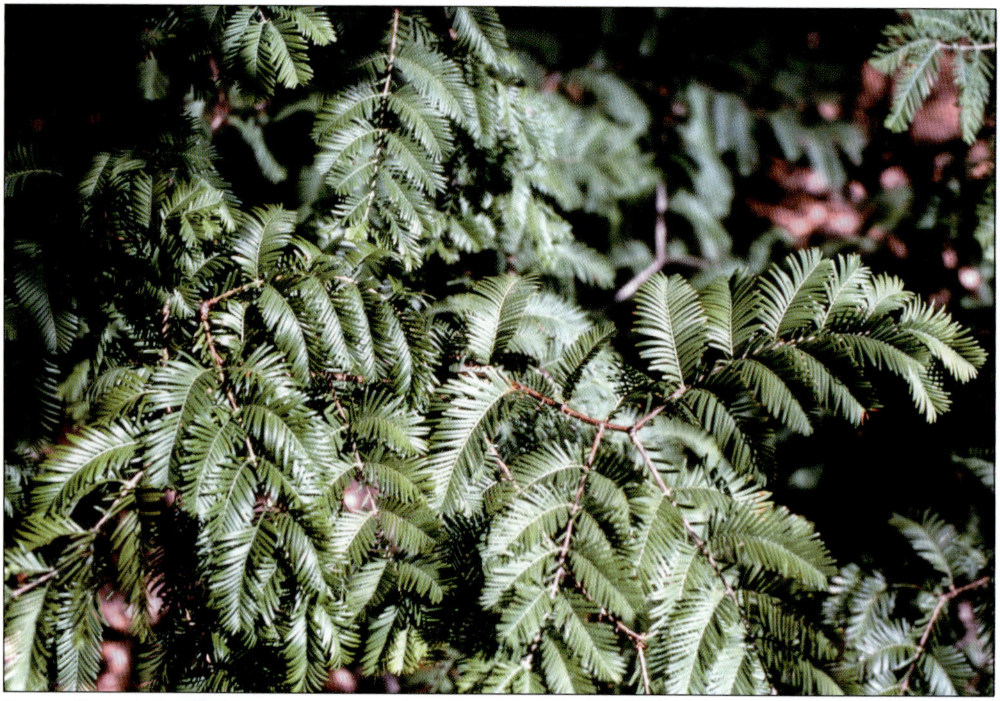

Dawn Redwood (*Metasequoia glyptostroboides*). One of the arboretum's most distinctive exotic trees is the dinosaur or fossil tree, a deciduous conifer with soft-to-the-touch needlelike leaves that turn an amber color in the autumn and drop to the ground. Thought to be extinct, the tree was discovered alive in its last living stand in southwestern China in 1941. In 1948, world distribution of the tree began when the Arnold Arboretum of Harvard University was one of the first to receive seeds from China. It promptly redistributed many of the seeds across the country, including to Dr. Bartlett. The arboretum has three majestic specimens, one of which was planted by Dr. Bartlett from the seeds he received in 1948; the other two are offspring of that tree. They grow fast and have been reported to reach 160 feet in height. (Below, courtesy of Dan Lenore.)

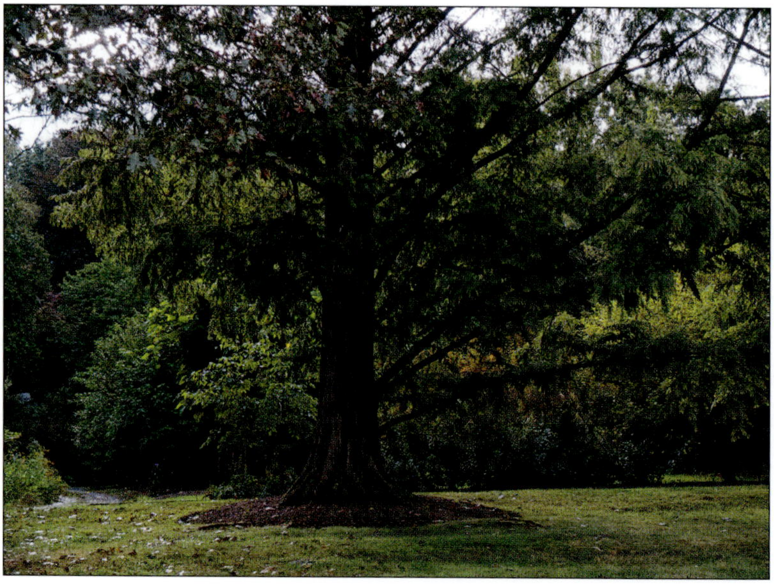

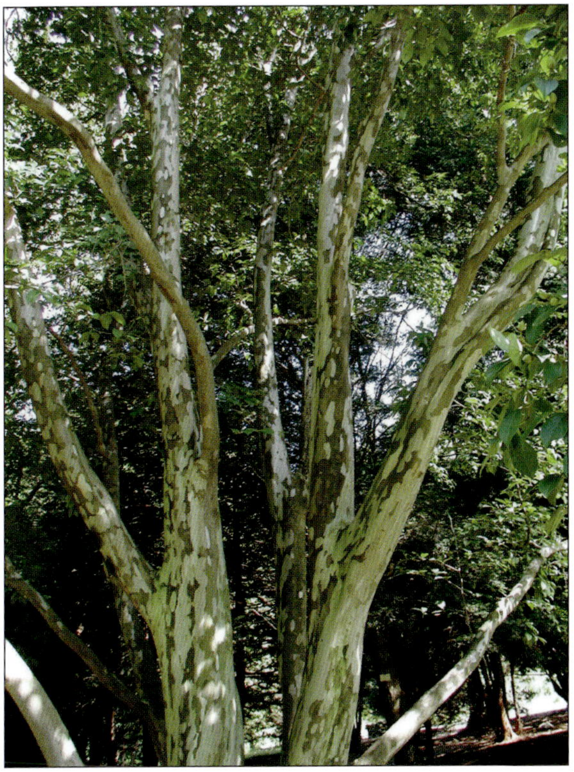

Korean Stewartia (*Stewartia koreana*). The arboretum's stewartia was a Connecticut Champion tree. Champion trees are quite old, which in some regions means 150 to 300 years, and the largest of their species. Because much of Connecticut was cleared for agricultural purposes in the 1880s, it is very hard to find trees older than 130 years in the region. Many of the trees at the arboretum have been considered champions over the years. The bark of this tree is unparalleled in its variety and coloring. (Courtesy of Dan Lenore.)

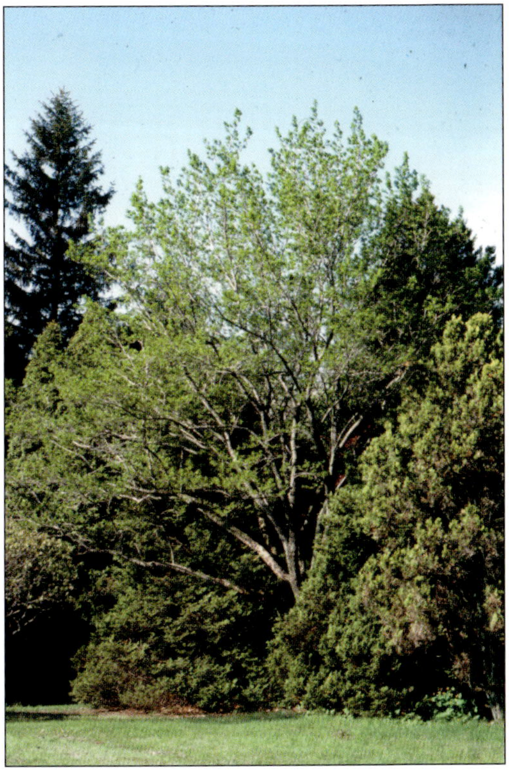

Hardy Rubber Tree (*Eucommia ulmoides*). Despite being native to China, this is an excellent medium-sized shade tree for the eastern United States, which is undoubtedly one of the reasons it attracted Dr. Bartlett's attention. It is pest-free, with shiny dark green leaves shaped like those of the elm tree (*Ulmus* spp.). It oozes a sticky, rubbery material when its leaves are torn. The arboretum's specimen was once named the Connecticut Champion for its species.

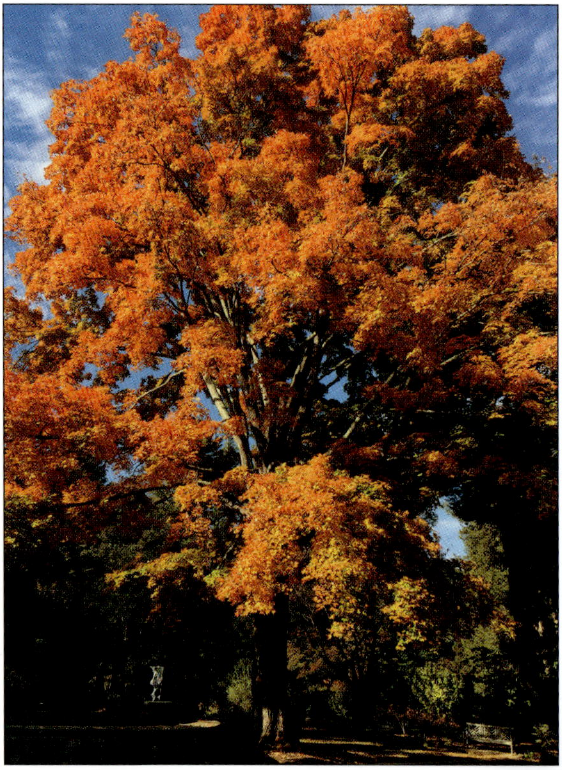

A Passion for Fruit, Nut, and Shade Trees. Dr. Bartlett's interest was not only for exotic trees from faraway places. He also had a deep passion for fruit, nut, and shade trees, whatever their origin. He understood not only the aesthetic value of trees, but also their commercial value. He worked with colleges, universities, government associations, horticultural, and agricultural organizations to research the impact of insects, disease, weather, and climate on the growth and viability of these trees. Many trees take decades to reach their full height and maturity. This means that collecting scientific data on the true impact of climate and disease on tree growth also takes decades. The arboretum has many very old specimens from Dr. Bartlett's early plantings and his experimentation over the years, the oldest of which are more than 100 years. Pictured at left is a sugar maple (*Acer saccharum*); below is a copper beech (*Fagus sylvatica*).

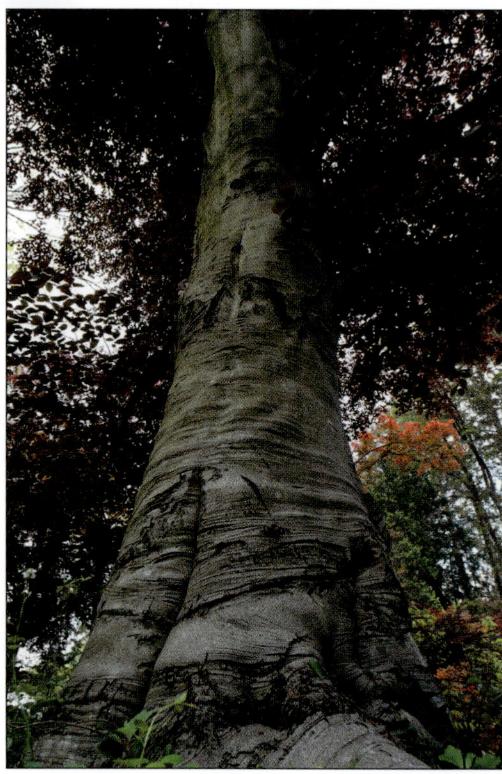

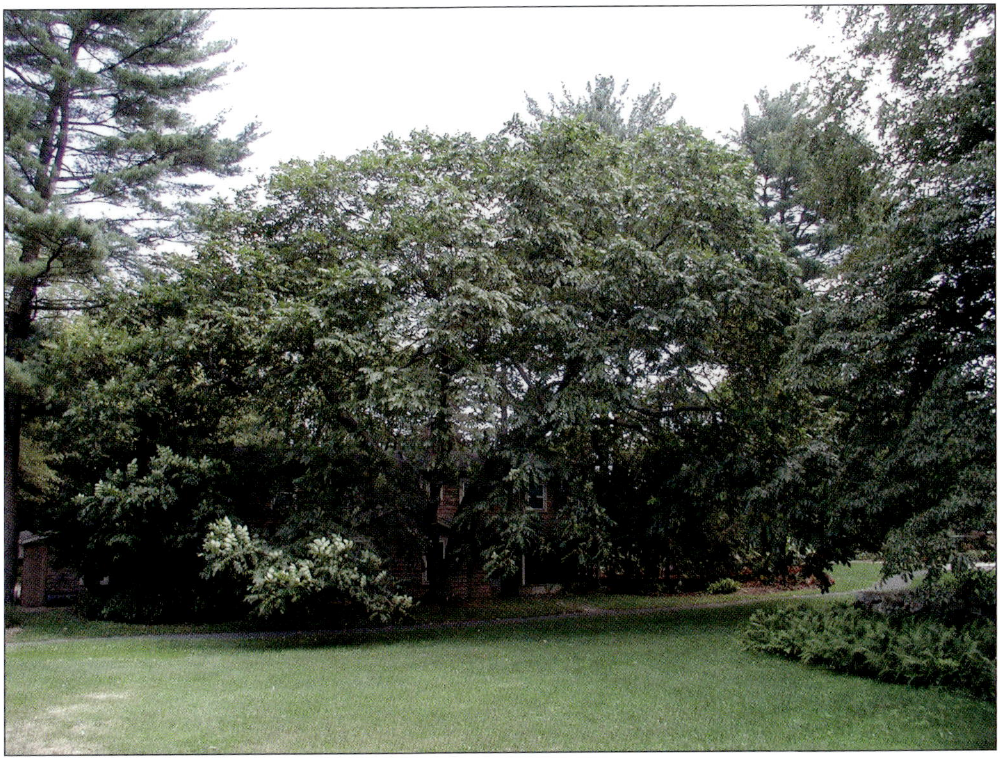

HEARTNUT (*JUGLANS AILANTHIFOLIA* VAR. *CORDIFORMIS*). This tree produces heart-shaped nuts that are buttery tasting and slightly sweet. This was a favorite in Dr. Bartlett's nut tree collection. One interesting fact about this tree is that on the first day that the temperature drops to freezing in the fall, most of its leaves drop at once, showering the arboretum for hours. It was at one time considered both a Connecticut and New England Champion.

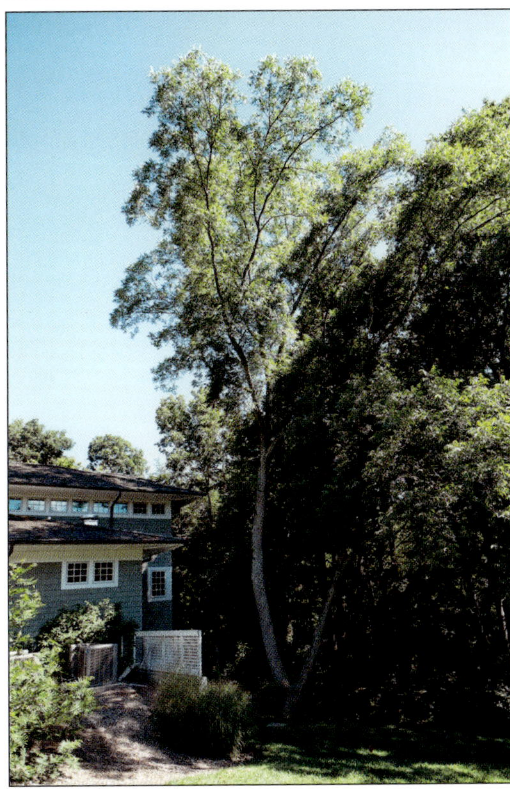

PECAN (*CARYA ILLINOINENSIS*). Living far outside of its comfortable hardiness zone, this southern nut-bearing tree withstood the severe cold of 1934, when the temperature dropped to minus 29° F, and of February 1948, when the temperature reached 25° below zero. While the tree has grown large here, the growing season in Connecticut is not long enough for the pecan nuts to mature. (Courtesy of Dan Lenore.)

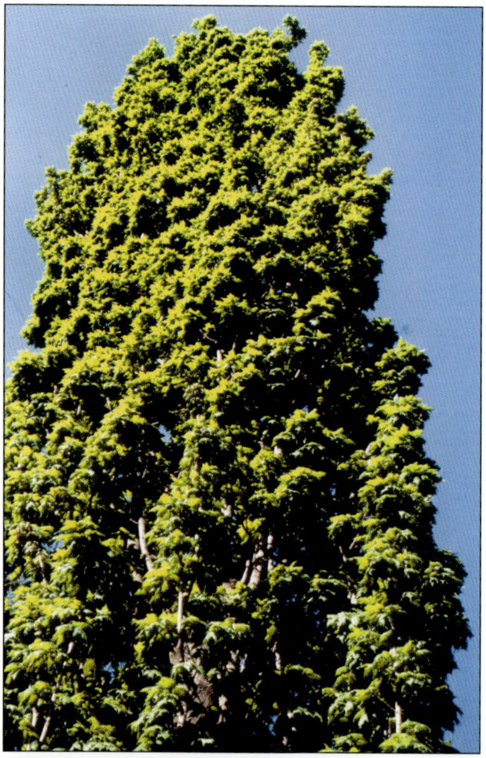

Sentry Sugar Maple (*Acer saccharum* 'Newton Sentry'). Its name comes from the fact that the first of its type was found near the entrance of Newton Cemetery in Newton, Massachusetts, in 1885. It is the narrowest of maples, the highest branches extending only a few feet out from the stem.

Franklin Tree (*Franklinia alatamaha*). As this tree is only marginally hardy in Connecticut, the arboretum tree has died back in certain winters, causing it to grow with multiple stems instead of a single trunk. John Bartram of Philadelphia supposedly collected the first seed for cultivation in 1770 near the Altamaha River in Georgia and named the tree for his friend Benjamin Franklin. It has gorgeous flowers.

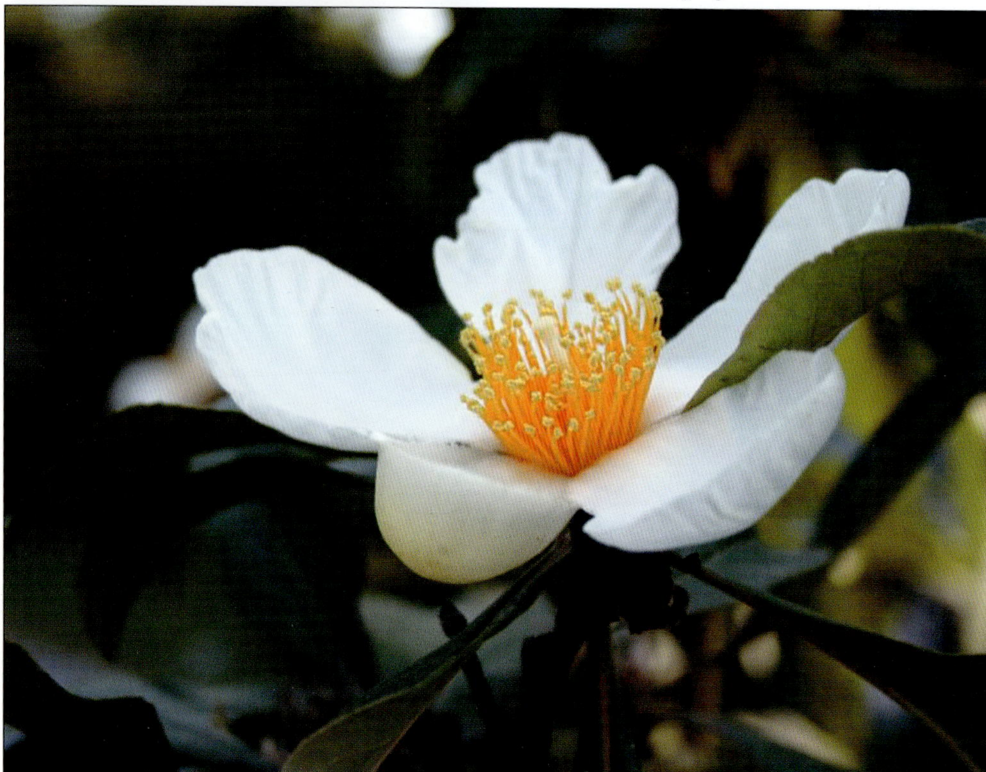

Eastern Redbud (*Cercis canadensis*). This favorite tree of Dr. Bartlett's, and many a visitor to the arboretum, is a relic that has outlived its normal lifespan; its now hollow main stem is hanging on for dear life. Graceful branching touches the earth from the divided stems that emerged close to the ground, providing a magnificent silhouette in all seasons for decades. Pink flowers signal the start of spring, closely followed by heart-shaped leaves, and finally yellow fall color. In 1998, the tree was named the "Bartlett King" in honor of Dr. Bartlett, who planted it in the 1940s, and was awarded champion status later. Arboretum staff will mourn the eventual passing of this tree, but have taken softwood cuttings from the "flags" it has pushed out trying to survive. In a few years, this fast-growing eastern US native will have many offspring to carry on its legacy. (Below, courtesy of Dan Lenore.)

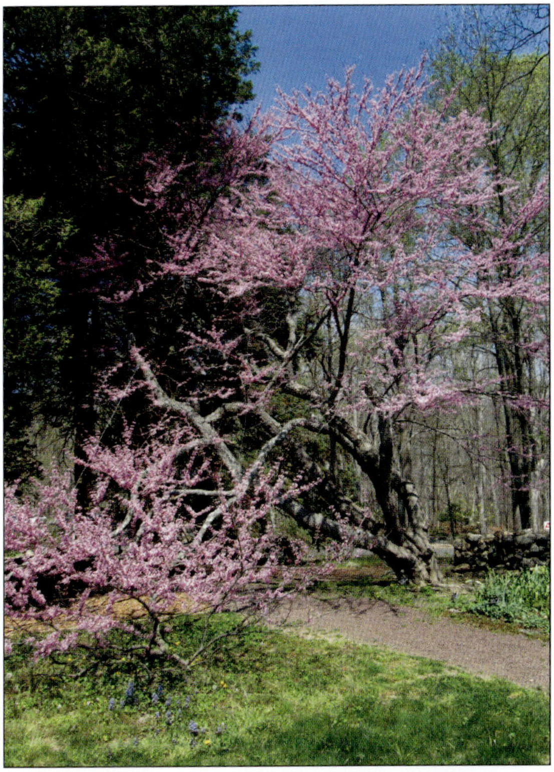

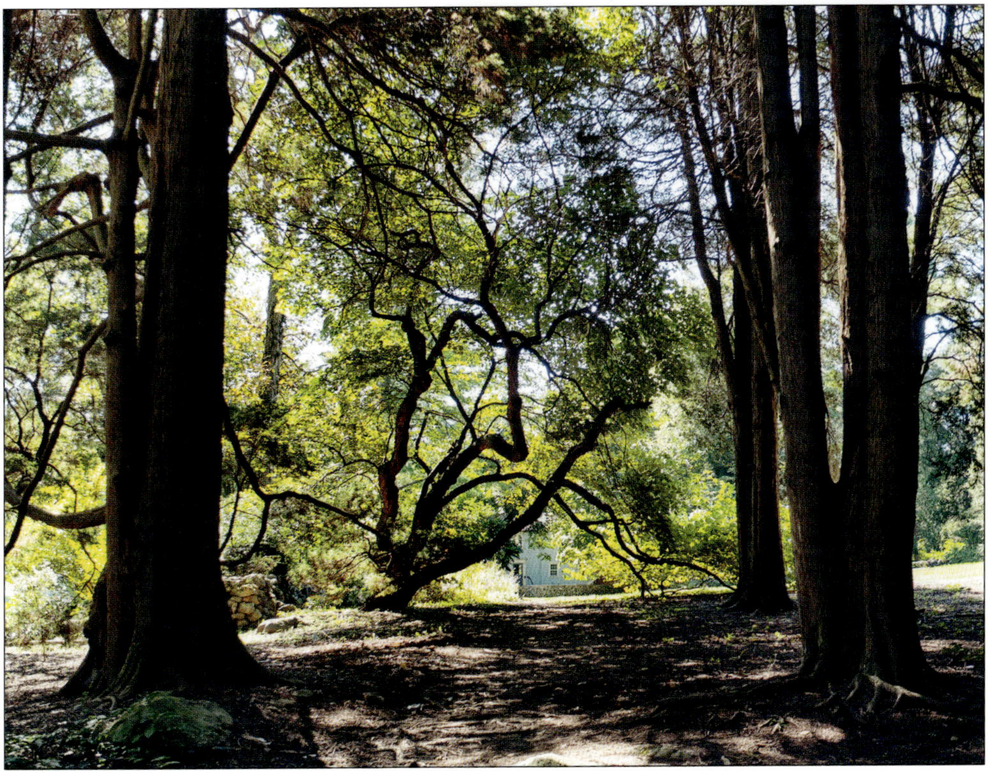

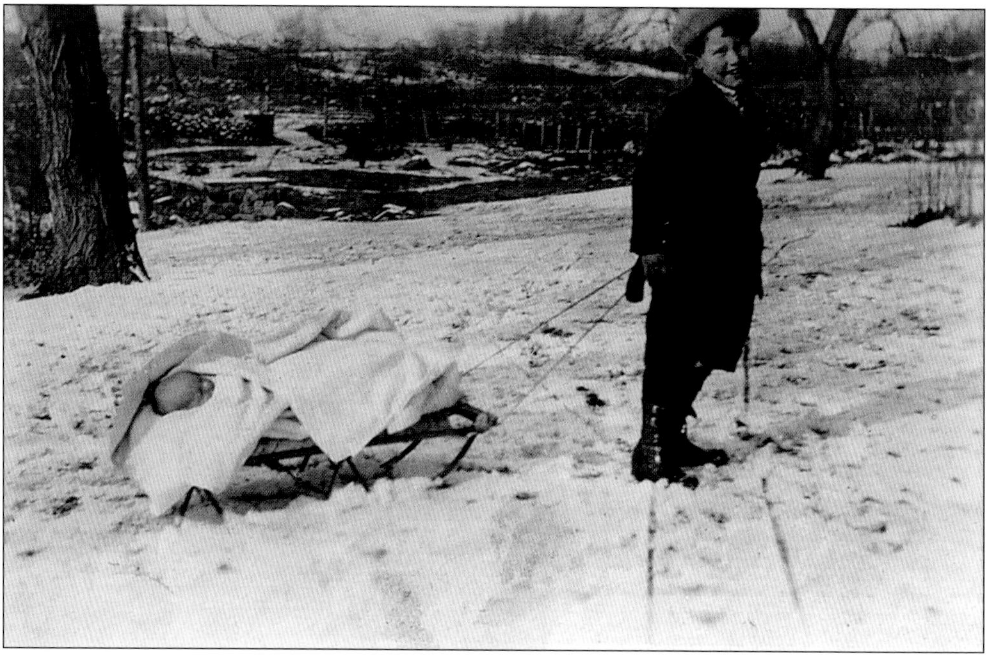

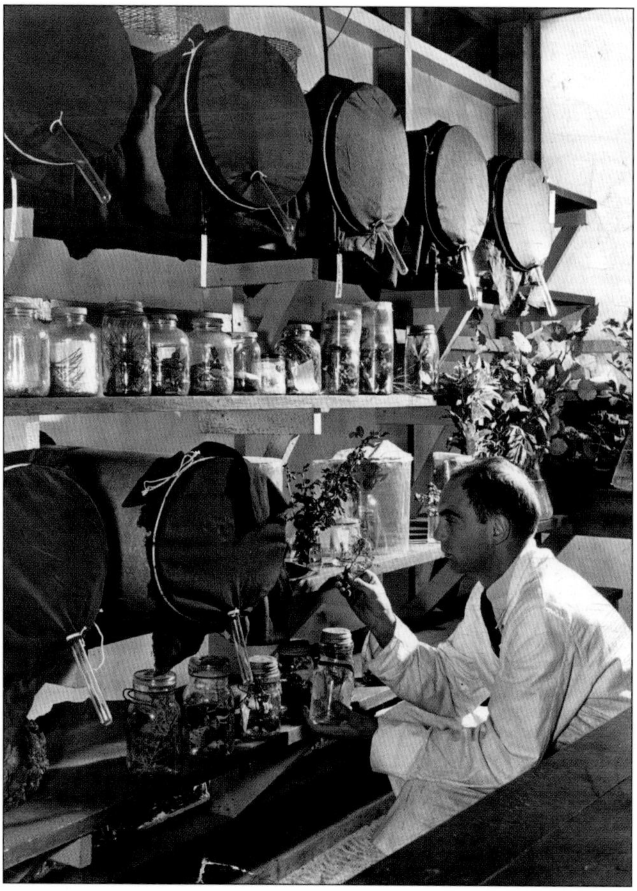

A New Beginning. Dr. Bartlett's children, Robert and Jane, grew up on the property (above). Robert (Robert Sr., left) entered his father's business. When Dr. Bartlett passed away on November 21, 1963, Robert Sr. decided that the company's research laboratory would be better located in a more favorable southern climate where many more species of plants could be grown. Accordingly, in 1965, the company purchased a tract of land in Charlotte, North Carolina, and began the process of moving the company's research activities there. However, that was not the end of the story for the arboretum. A group of dedicated men and women took up the cause of preserving a part of the property as public, open space. It is a story of how the government, the Bartlett family, and ordinary citizens came together to create the arboretum as it exists today. (Both, courtesy of The F.A. Bartlett Tree Expert Company.)

Two

THE BLOSSOMING OF THE ARBORETUM

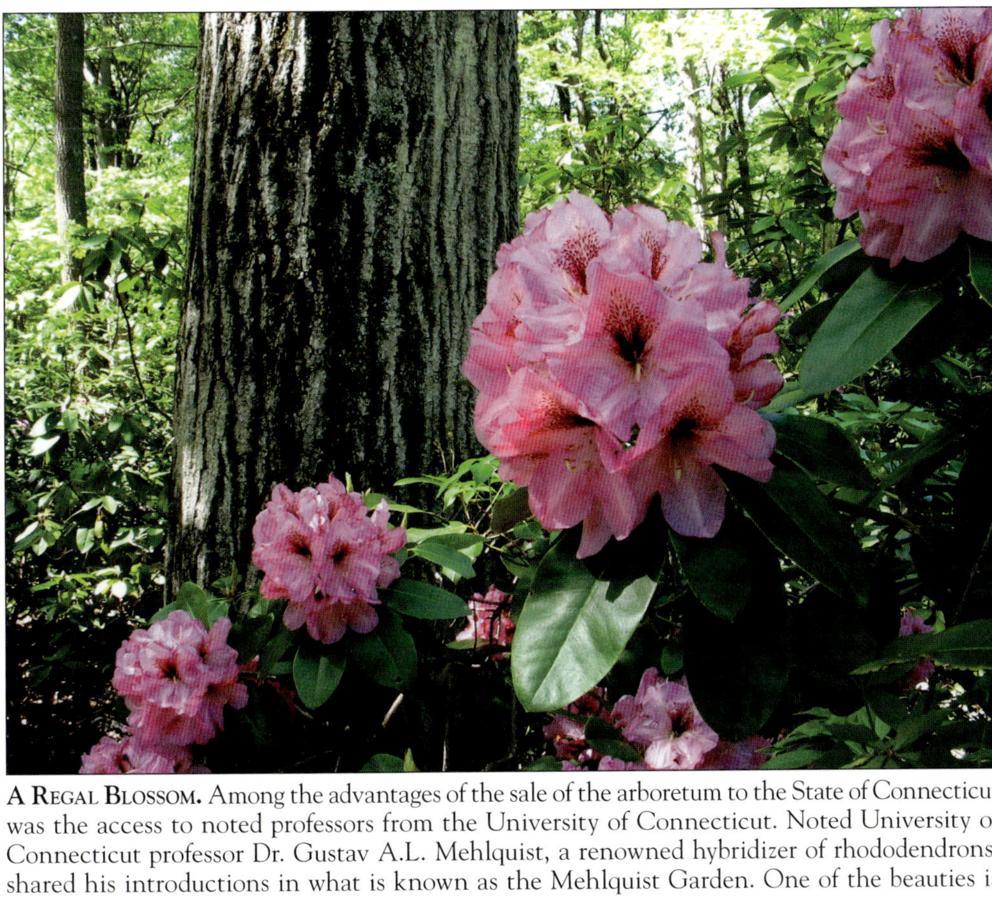

A REGAL BLOSSOM. Among the advantages of the sale of the arboretum to the State of Connecticut was the access to noted professors from the University of Connecticut. Noted University of Connecticut professor Dr. Gustav A.L. Mehlquist, a renowned hybridizer of rhododendrons, shared his introductions in what is known as the Mehlquist Garden. One of the beauties is pictured here.

THE BARTLETT ARBORETUM

OF THE

STATE OF CONNECTICUT

Brookdale Road

Stamford, Conn.

ARBORETUM COMMITTEE

Chairman

Booth Hemingway

Vice Chairmen

Malcolm J. Edgerton, Jr.

Henry C. Niewenhous

Bradley A. Walker

Advertising

Bradley A. Walker

Art Director

Jack E. Brown

Garden Clubs

Mrs. James E. Hubbell

Area Chairmen

Danbury

Mrs. Frederick F. Robinson

Darien

John Oldrin

Fairfield-Bridgeport

Mrs. Alice Orme Smith

Greenwich

Joseph A. Dietrich

Hartford

Mrs. John D. Britton

Litchfield

Gordon Loery

New Canaan

Henry A. Caesar II

New Haven

Kimberly Cheney

Westport-Weston

Thaddeus G. Cowell, Jr.

New London

Mrs. Chester W. Kitchings

Meridan

Roy Wilcox

Ridgefield

Mr. & Mrs. Daniel M. McKeon

Stamford

Mrs. Jonathan Lanman

Torrington

Mrs. Rea King McCarty

Washington

Edmund K. Swigart

December 15, 1965

Dear Friend:

You will be pleased to learn that The Bartlett Arboretum is now the property of the State of Connecticut.

This is due, in part, to your generous response to our appeal. Without the help of people such as you, the opportunity to preserve this property for the future would have been lost.

A group of us are now working with the State as private individuals to lay out a plan for the improvement and development of the entire area. We hope to be able to keep you informed of the progress as we go along.

If all goes well, the Arboretum will be open to everyone in the late Spring. We hope to see you then.

Sincerely yours,

Booth Hemingway
Chairman

GRASSROOTS EFFORT GROWS TO TRY AND PRESERVE THE PROPERTY. An Arboretum Committee was formed by concerned citizens to raise funds to purchase a portion of the Bartlett estate for use as a public arboretum. The *Stamford Advocate* reported on December 20, 1965, that the Arboretum Committee had adopted as its theme the phrase "A Reverence for Wood," the title of a book by writer and illustrator Eric Sloane. This theme captured the passion of the committee members for preservation of natural wooded areas. The committee's efforts were successful and would be further rewarded in 1980 when local residents Mr. and Mrs. Dwight Marshall transferred two additional acres of land connecting the arboretum property to the Stamford Museum and Nature Center. With this two-acre link, a greenway from the southern border of the arboretum to the northern border of the Stamford Museum and Nature Center was established.

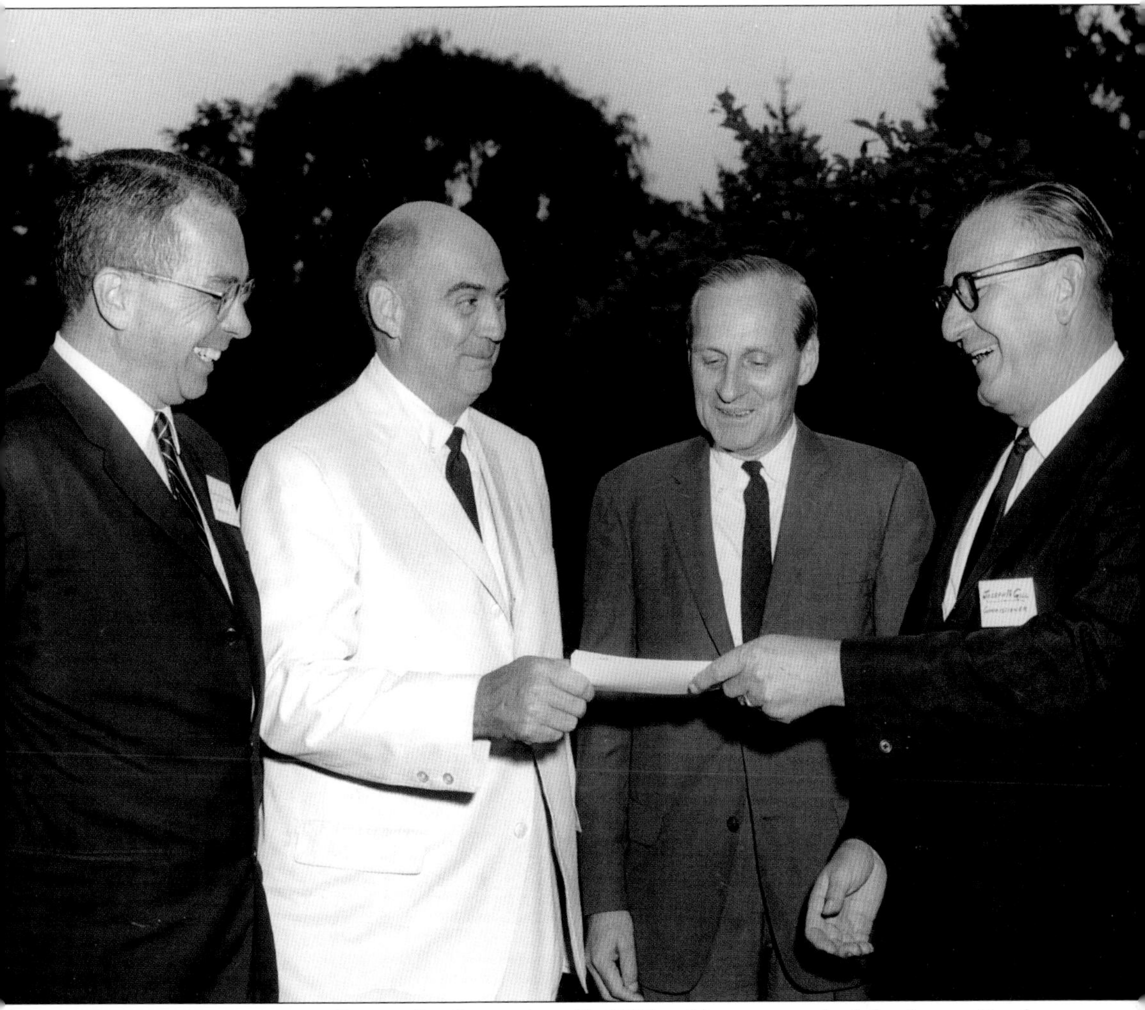

A Public Arboretum is Born. On September 19, 1965, a 64-acre parcel of the former Bartlett Tree Research Laboratories was transferred from the Bartlett family to the State of Connecticut to be used as an arboretum open to the public for research, education, and enjoyment of the natural environment. Pictured here are, from left to right, Booth Hemingway, chairman of the Arboretum Committee, which spearheaded the raising of funds for the purchase of the arboretum property; Robert Bartlett Sr., son of Francis A. Bartlett; Thomas Mayers, mayor of Stamford; and Joseph N. Gill, Connecticut state commissioner of agriculture and natural resources. The arboretum would be named in honor of Francis Bartlett. Upon completion of the transfer, the property was operated under a public-private partnership between the state and the newly formed Bartlett Arboretum Association Inc.

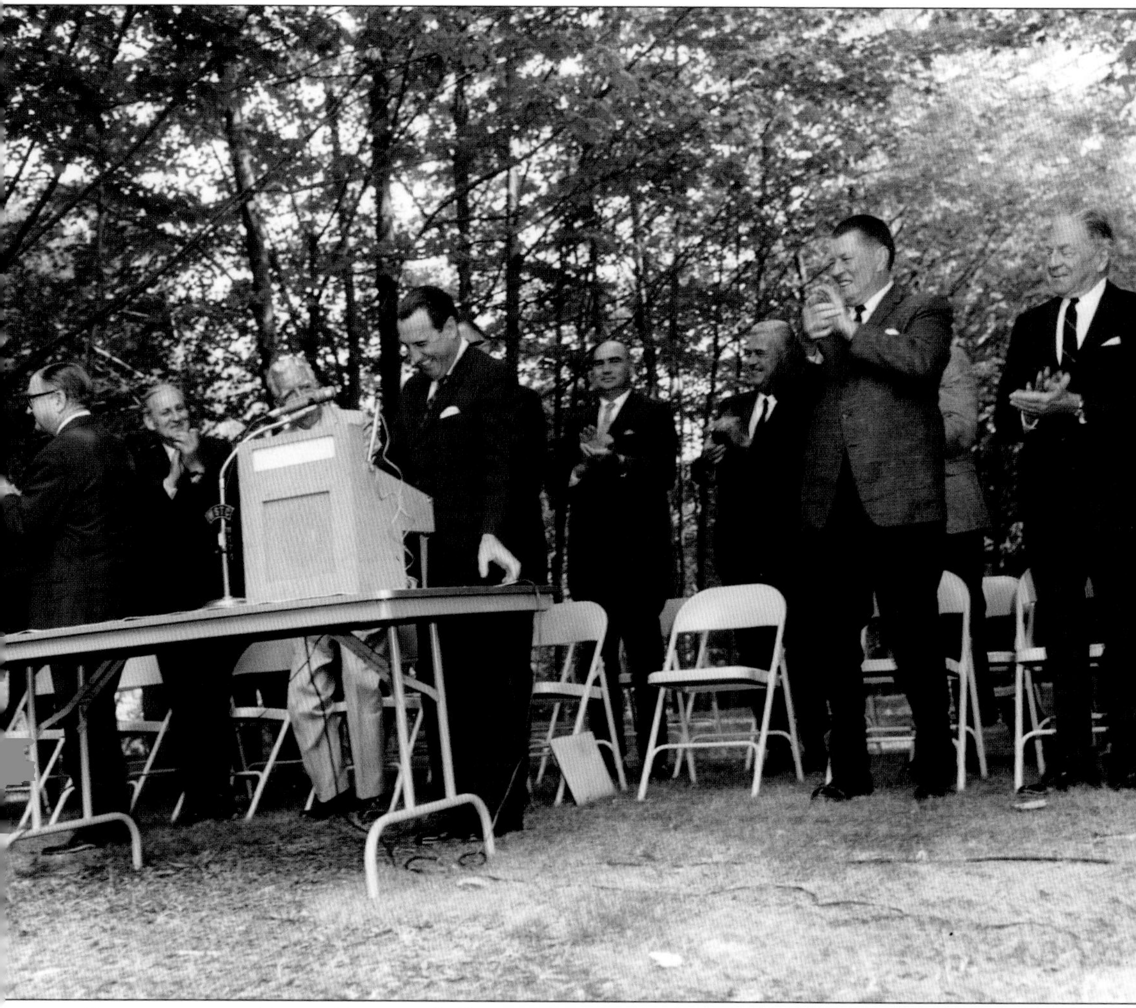

DEDICATION AND PUBLIC OPENING. In September 1966, almost a year after the transfer, the arboretum was dedicated as a public arboretum under the jurisdiction of the Connecticut Department of Environmental Protection. State and federal funds under the Open Spaces Program provided the majority of the financing for the purchase price. Many government officials attended the dedication. Shown here is Connecticut's 81st governor, John N. Dempsey, at the podium during the dedication. Sen. Abe Ribicoff and Stamford mayor Thomas Mayer also attended. Robert Bartlett Sr. can be seen in the second row behind Governor Dempsey. The Connecticut Department of Environmental Protection assigned responsibility for operating the arboretum to the Department of Plant Science of the University of Connecticut. The Bartlett Arboretum Association partnered with the Department of Plant Science through the establishment of a joint board of overseers to plan and develop the arboretum as a living museum.

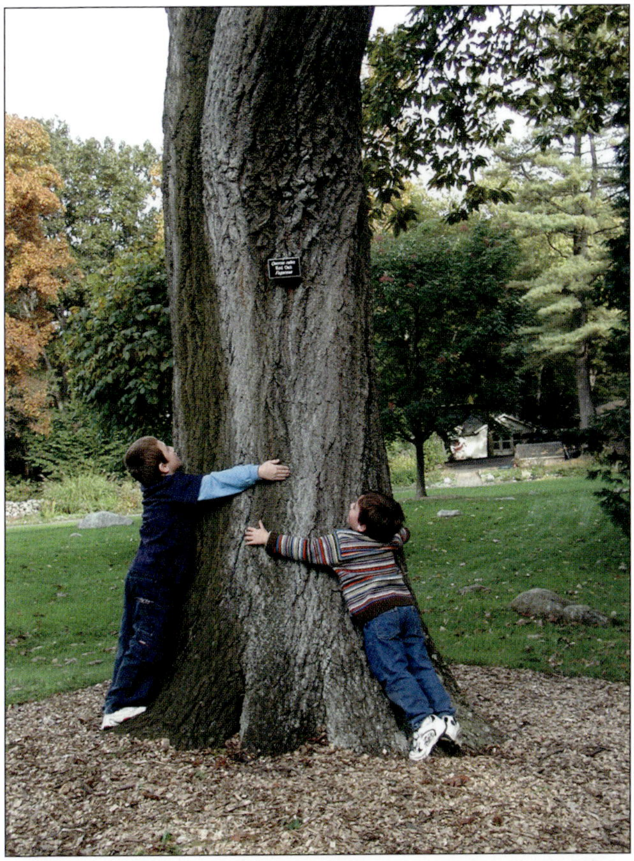

More Than a Park. According to the *Stamford Advocate* on November 23, 1965, at the time of the transfer of the property, there were approximately 800 specimens of "some of the most unusual trees, shrubs, and plants in the world." The goal of those who came together to save a portion of the property as a public arboretum was that it could be run with the dual purpose of providing an open space for public access to nature, as well as a place for scientific research and education for both children and adults, leveraging the work begun by Dr. Bartlett, the Bartlett Tree Research Laboratories, and the School of Tree Surgery.

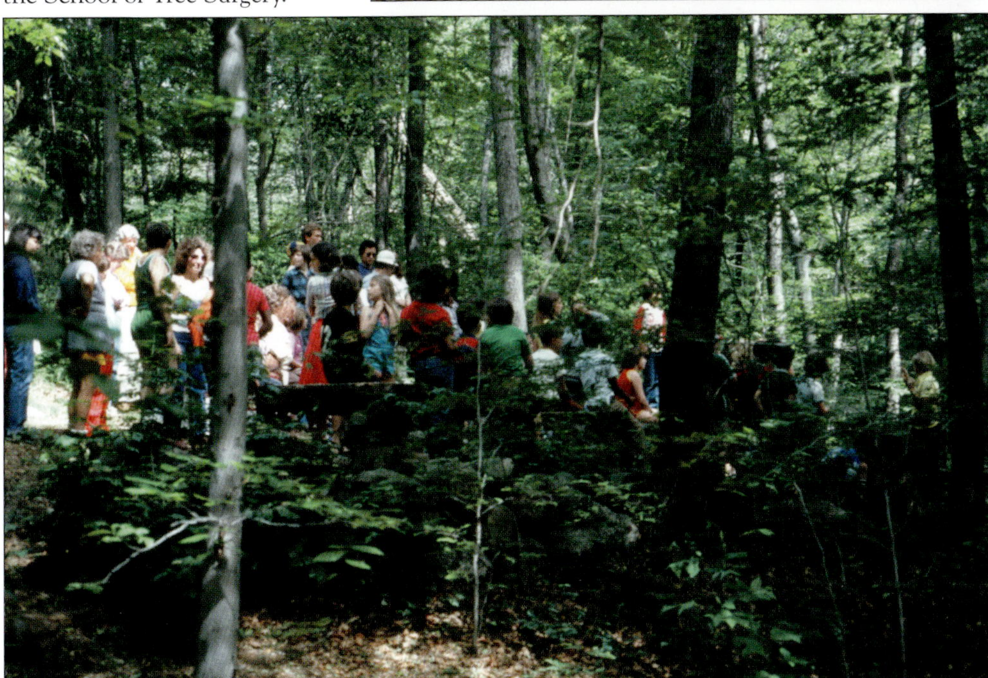

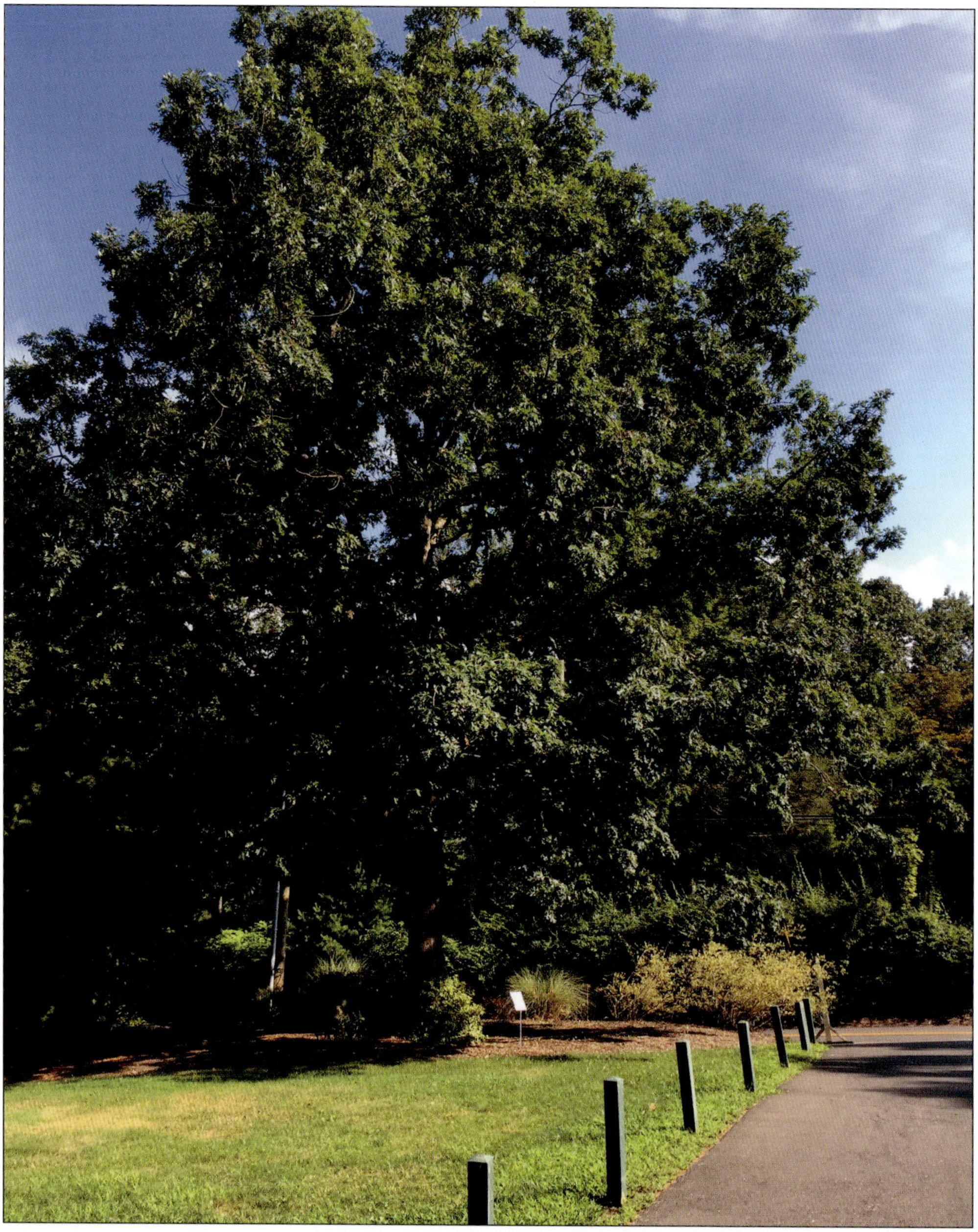

"Charter Oak" (*Quercus alba*). This white oak on the arboretum property is a descendant of Connecticut's Charter Oak. The seedling of this historically significant tree was obtained more than 50 years ago by Dorothy Lozenzon upon attending the Constitutional Convention of Connecticut in 1965. The Connecticut Royal Charter issued by King Charles II established Connecticut's independence. According to legend, following Charles's death, his brother King James II ascended the throne and disapproved of royal charters. He demanded that Connecticut surrender its charter. As the story goes, Capt. Joseph Wadsworth hid the charter in the hollow of a nearby oak tree. Freedom was saved, and the constitution was upheld. The Charter Oak was estimated to be 1,000 years old when it finally fell in 1856, a testimony to the strength and endurance of the mighty oak tree.

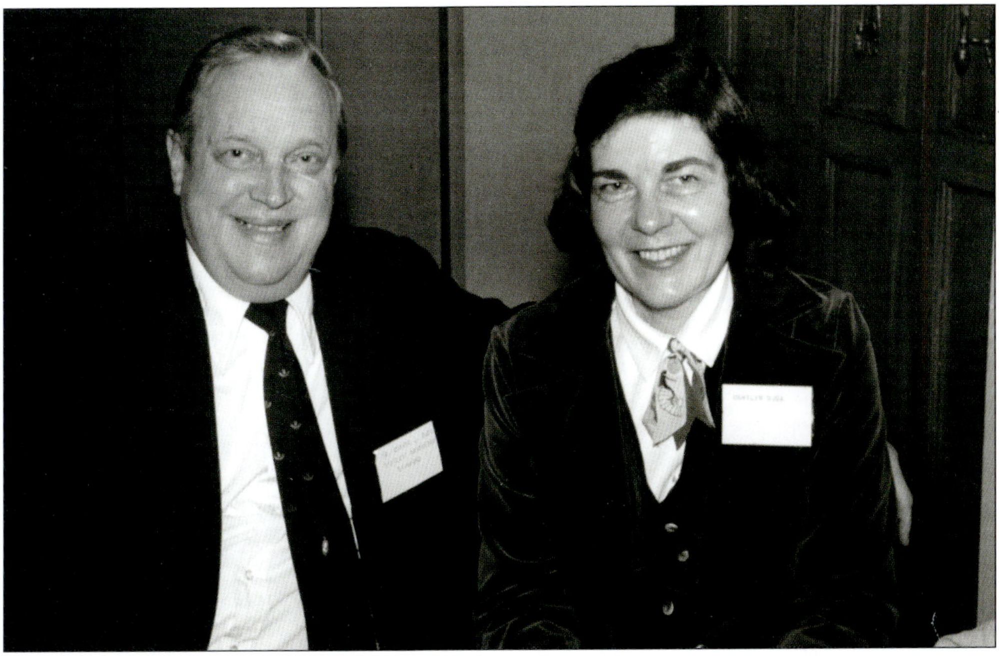

Dr. Edward Duda Named First Director. Dr. Edward J. Duda, pictured here with his wife, became the first director of the arboretum. Dr. Duda had a long history with the property, having worked at the arboretum as an entomologist for Bartlett Tree Research Laboratories since 1951. Dr. Duda received his bachelor of science degree from the New York State College of Forestry in Syracuse in 1948 and his master of science and doctorate in entomology from the University of Massachusetts. Under Dr. Duda's leadership, the arboretum would focus on several themes that still resonate today—horticulture education for the public, scientific research, and the support of public school education, both through direct education of students as well as training of area educators in ecology and the natural environment. Duda remained at the arboretum as its well-respected director until his death in 1979; a bench was dedicated in his memory.

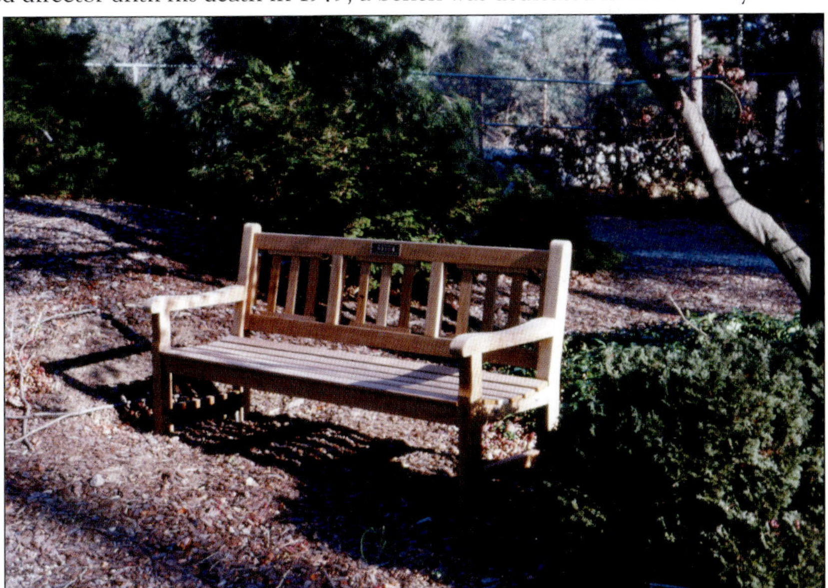

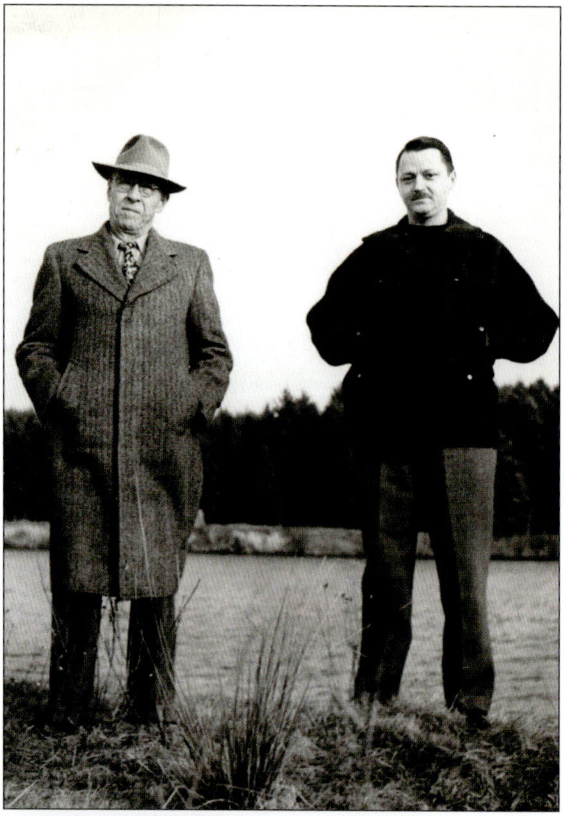

Merging of Personnel. In addition to Dr. Duda, the new arboretum retained the services of two others from the Bartlett Tree Research Laboratories, groundskeeper Dick Marino and secretary Gaye Mote (below, right). They would both stay with the arboretum for decades and were joined by University of Connecticut faculty and staff. One of the first to join the arboretum was Dr. Philip G. Rusden (left, at left), associate professor of plant science. He became the first director of education programs. Together, Dr. Duda and Dr. Rusden started many public educational programs, including a plant clinic open from May to September to provide advice to the public on plant diseases and insects. A version of this plant clinic exists today at the arboretum.

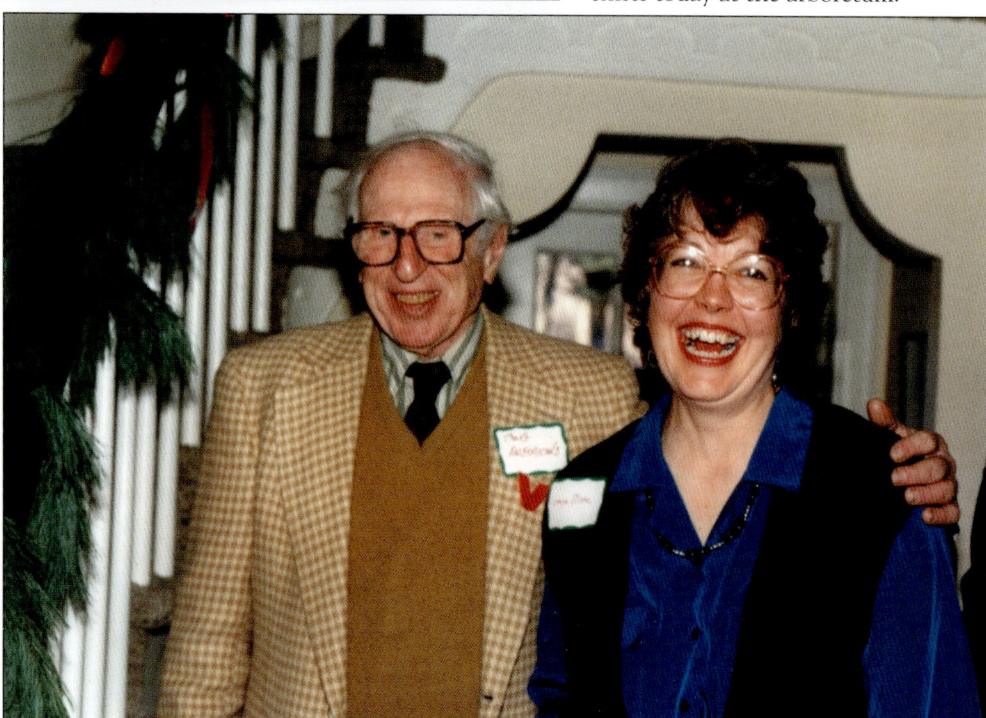

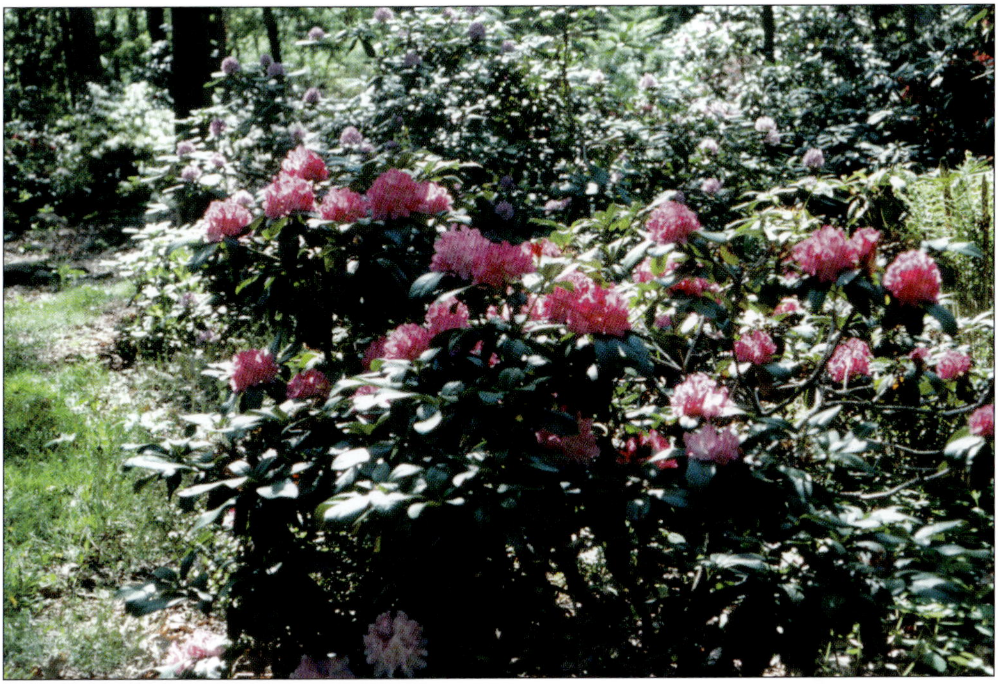

DR. MEHLQUIST BRINGS RHODODENDRON EXPERTISE FROM STORRS. Dr. Gustav A.L. Mehlquist, professor of plant breeding and biology at the University of Connecticut in Storrs, was active at the arboretum in establishing the first ericaceous area (plants in the heath or heather family that grow in acidic and infertile soils) planted in 1966 and 1967. He was well known for his work in breeding hybrid rhododendrons and azaleas. The arboretum benefitted greatly from his work, as he provided many of the specimens of rhododendrons planted here. Dr. Mehlquist stayed active at the arboretum even after becoming a professor emeritus at the University of Connecticut. (Below, courtesy of Dan Lenore.)

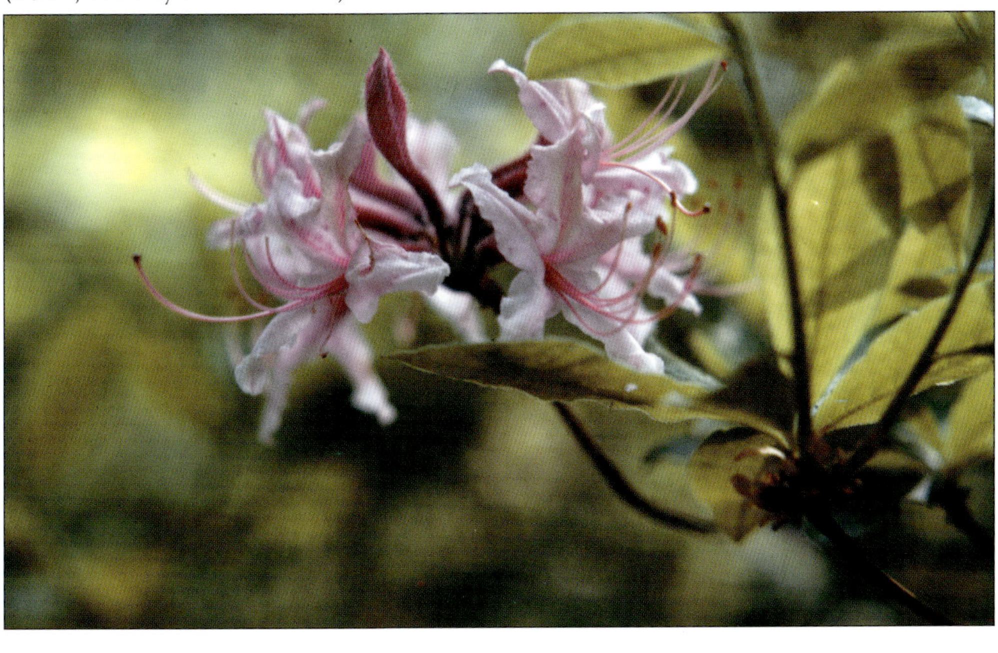

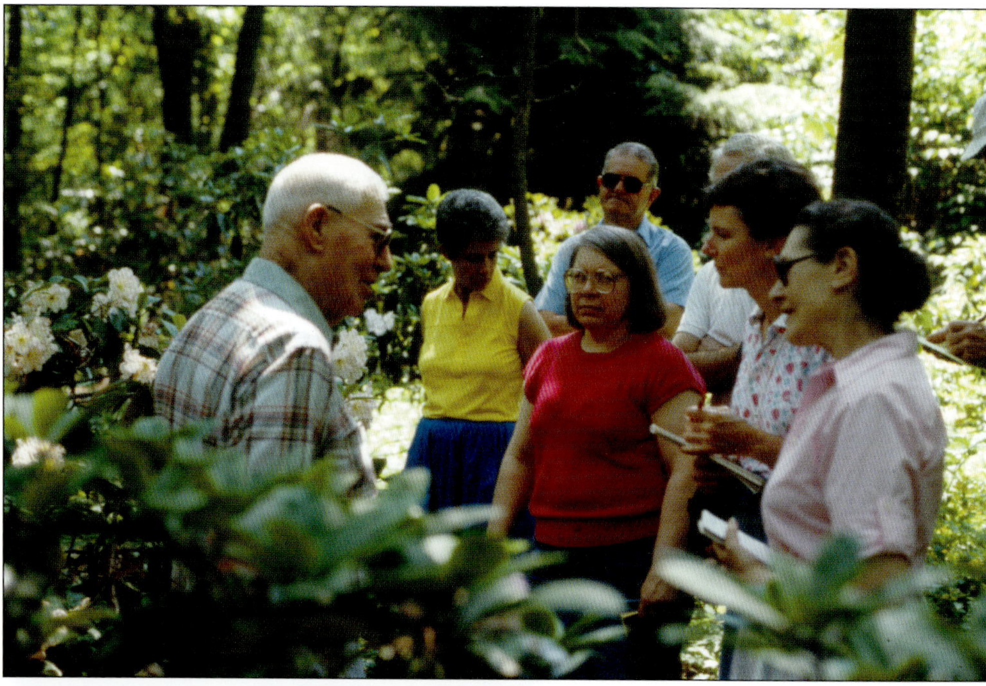

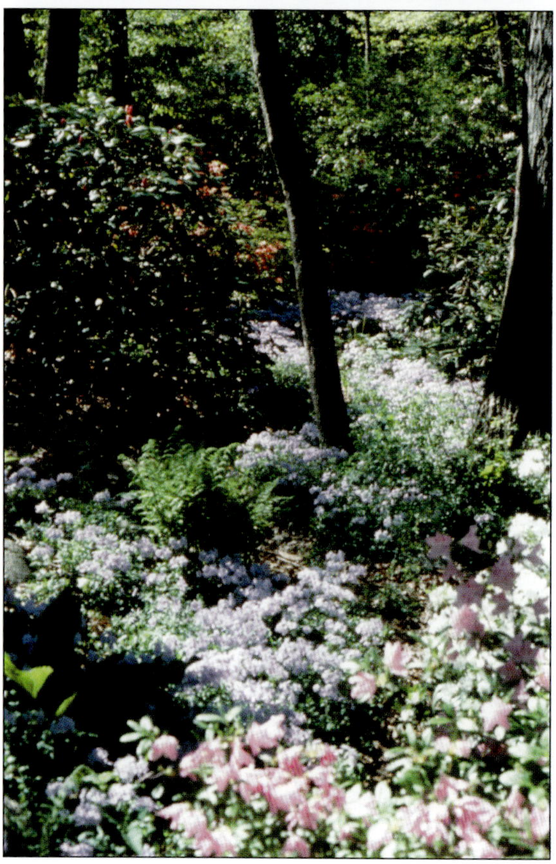

A Walk in Honor of Dr. Mehlquist. In his later years, Dr. Mehlquist could be seen at the arboretum, particularly in the Rhododendron Garden, for annual Sunday tours. The Bartlett Arboretum newsletter for the fall of 1977 describes a tour led by a 71-year-old Dr. Mehlquist in which he shared his observations on gardening, horticulture, and rhododendrons. Some favorite Mehlquist quips include: "The successful gardener is one who never has enough space; those who do aren't successful. . . . In horticulture rarely does one carry something from beginning to completion. . . . A rhododendron grown in full sun has more blossoms but a briefer bloom, while a rhododendron grown in the shade has fewer blossoms but a longer bloom."

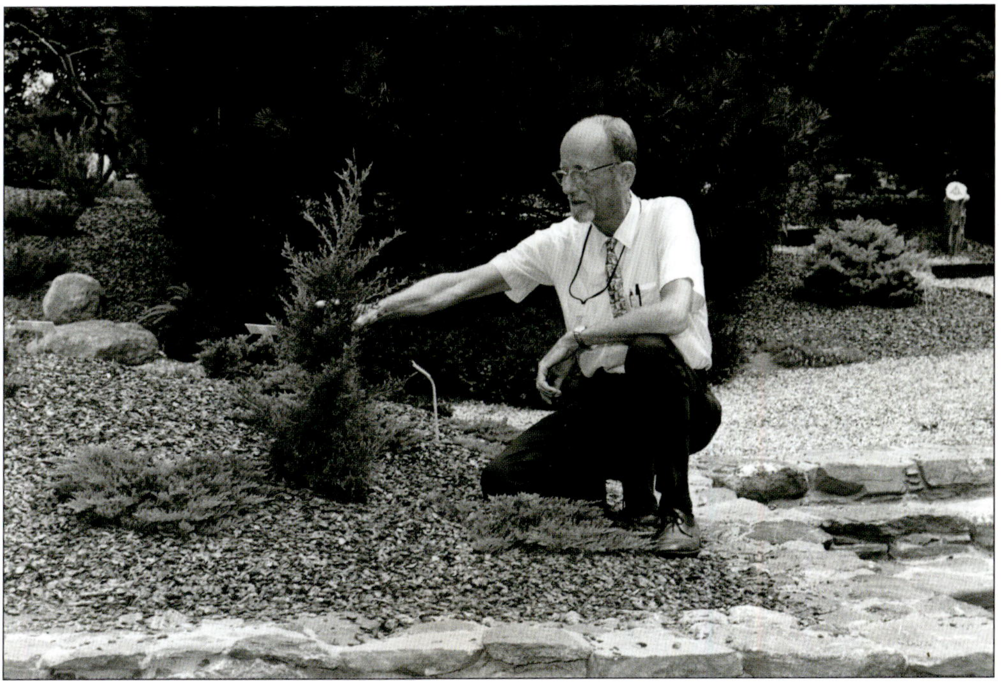

Seth Kelsey Joins the Arboretum. Upon the retirement of Dr. Rusden in 1971, Seth Kelsey joined the arboretum staff as a horticulturist. Kelsey would be instrumental in working with Dr. Mehlquist on the planting of the ericaceous area. Kelsey was also key in transforming the Bartlett family rock garden into a dwarf conifer garden, situated on about an acre across Brookdale Road in front of the Homestead. Pictured above is Kelsey examining a juniper in the arboretum's new Dwarf Conifer Garden in 1972. Below is the Dwarf Conifer Garden as it continued to expand.

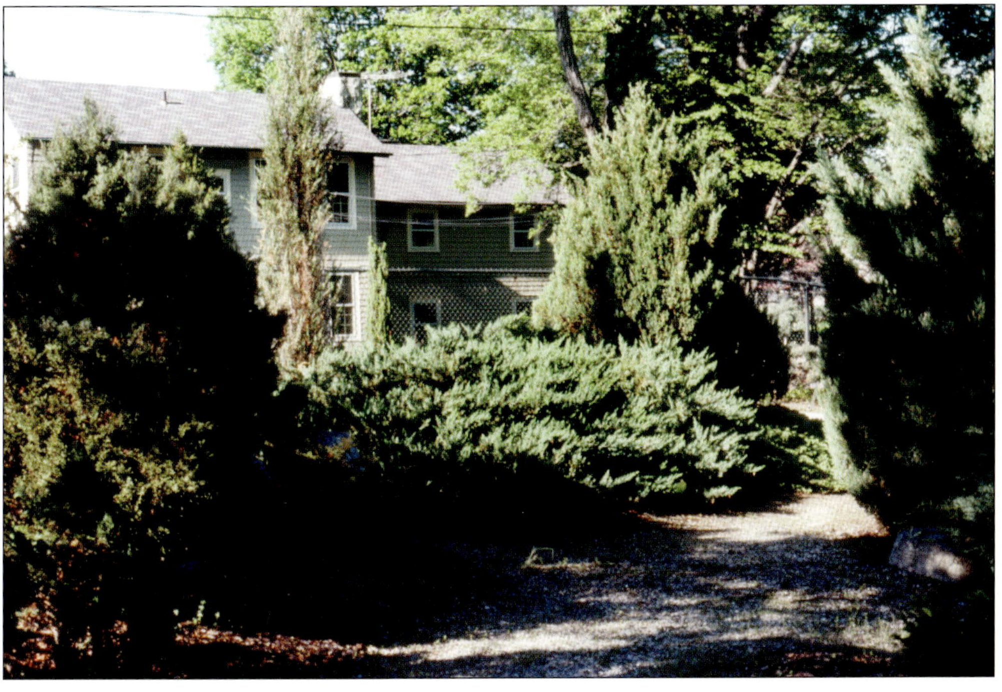

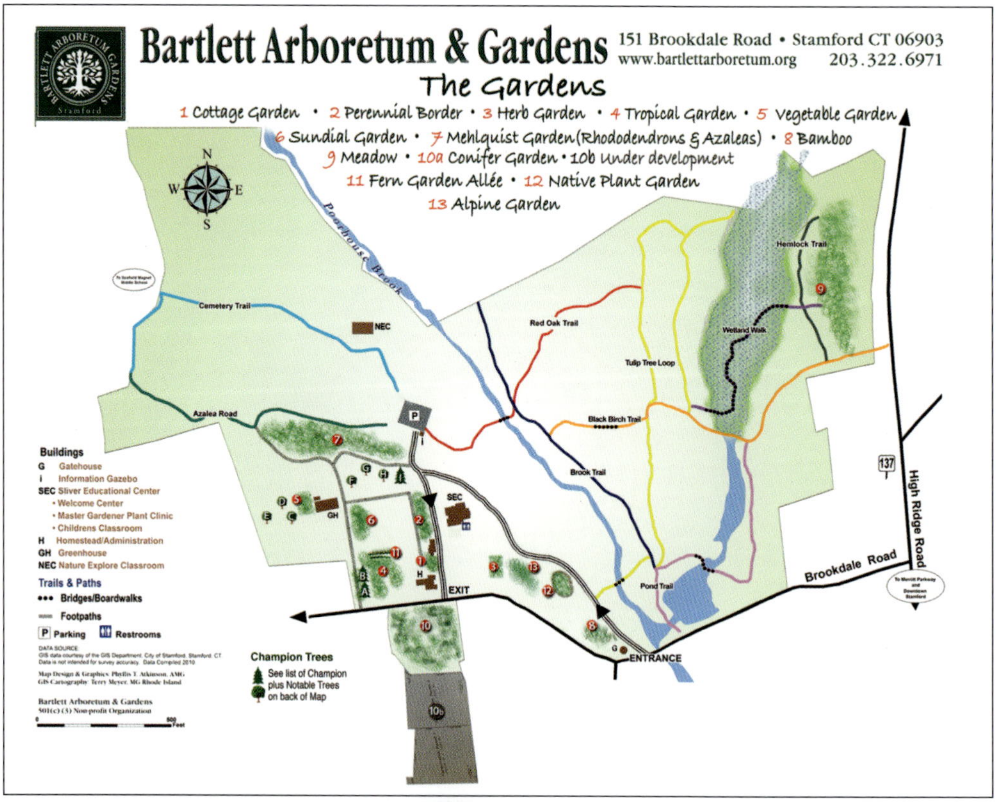

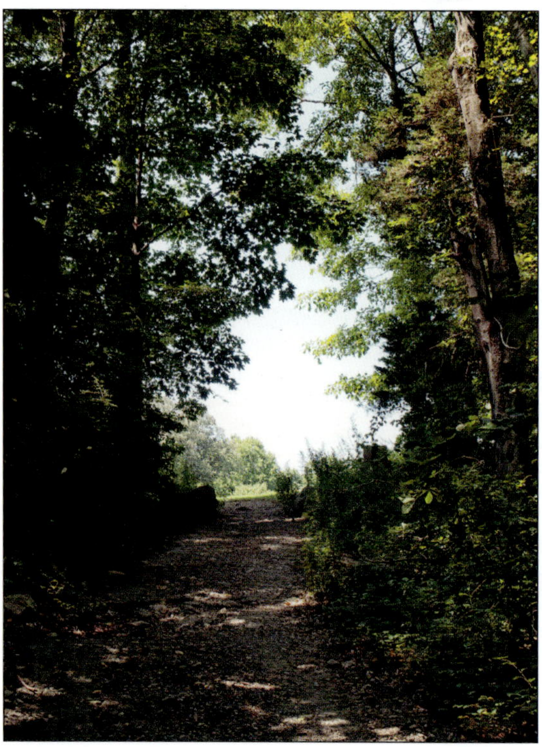

Creating Trails for Public Use. As the property transitioned from a private to a public arboretum, a trail system was established in the natural wooded areas for ease of access. Over five miles of trails were created and mapped so that visitors could "lose" themselves in the natural forested areas. As part of the educational programs, and in an effort to educate visitors on what they could observe as they walked the trails, a guides program was created in 1969 under the direction of volunteer Rose Thielens. Docents led hundreds of walks describing the historical features, habitat, geology, watershed, and plant life along the trails. There were also printed guides that visitors could use. Docent-led tours are still provided today, as well as a free touring app available for download on cell phones (BartlettArb). (Above, courtesy of Phyllis Atkinson.)

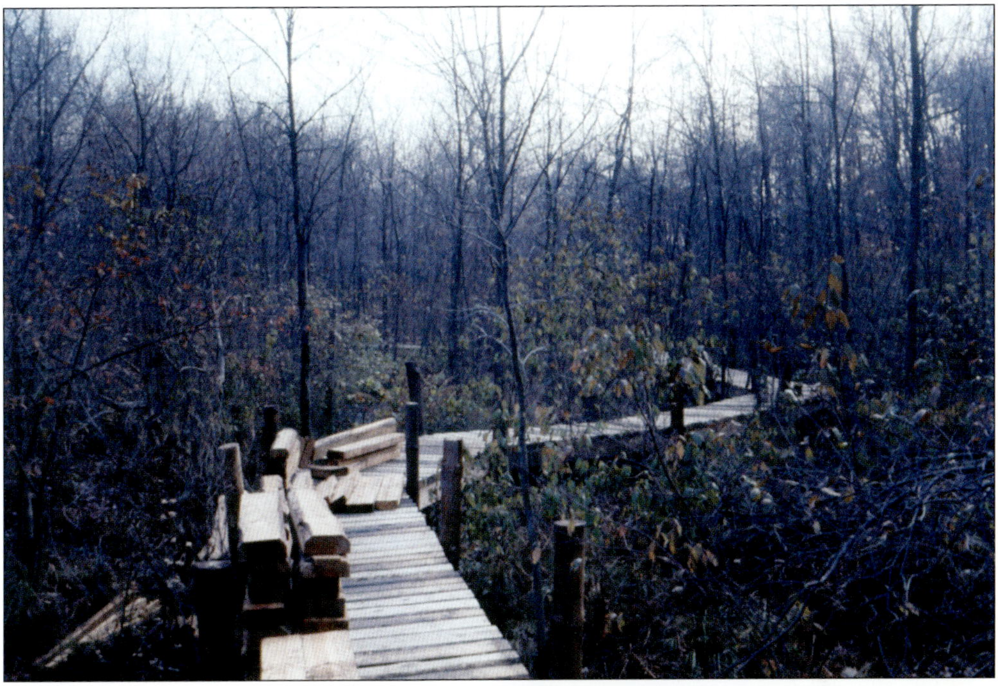

Bog Walk Created as Part of Trail System. Local Girl Scout Troop 57 worked from 1969 to 1971 to build an elevated 1,000-foot bog walk through the woodland swamp of the arboretum. The Girl Scouts were assisted by Boy Scout Explorer Post 76. Dr. Duda and Dr. Rusden designed and supervised the project, assisted by arboretum staff. On view from the boardwalk is the vibrant ecological environment so different from the surrounding woodland. The Bartlett swamp contains a rare treasure of red maples (*Acer rubrum*) of many sizes and shapes. In the fall, the orange and yellow leaves of the maples are contrasted with the deep red leaves of the blackgum (*Nyssa sylvatica*) trees adjacent to the boardwalk. The swamp is also a habitat for tadpoles, bullfrogs, ducks, hawks, and other wildlife.

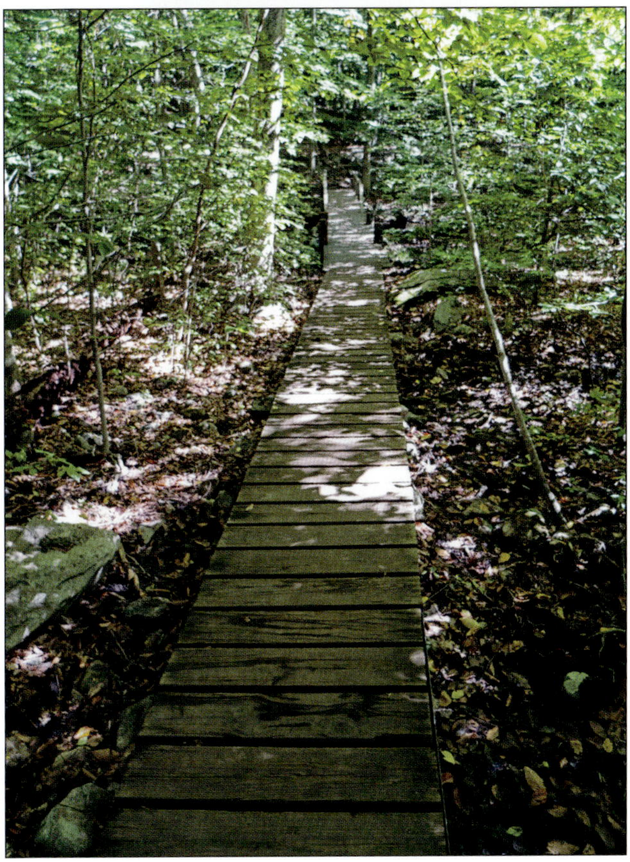

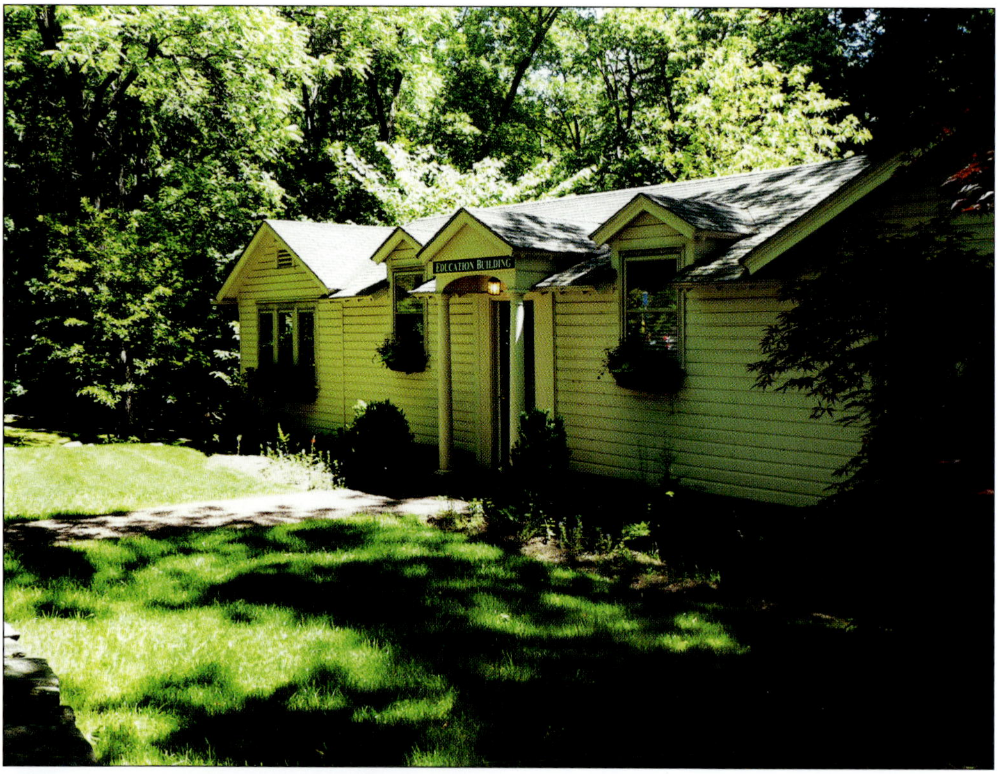

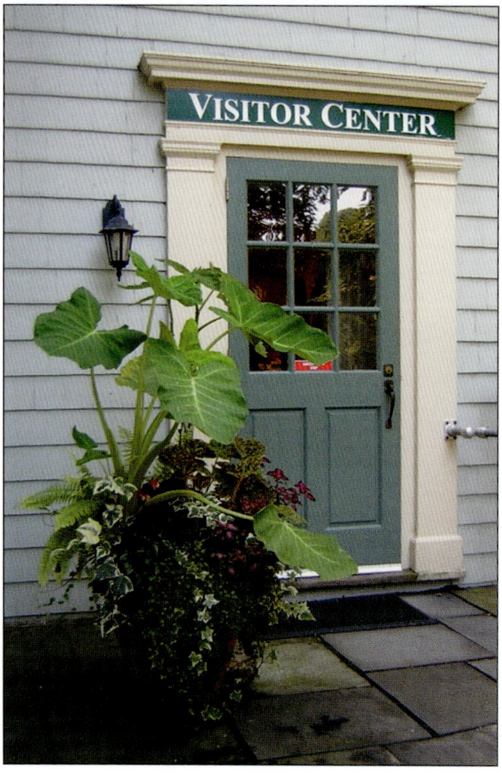

Improvements for Public Use and Enjoyment. As part of the transition to a public space, the buildings at the arboretum were repurposed for administrative offices, education, and public access. The Stone Laboratory became the Education Center and Herbarium and was the focus for arboretum educational offerings to adult gardeners and students who visited with their schools. The Homestead became administrative offices and a visitor center. Forsyth Laboratory became a warming hut for those who skated on Forsyth Pond in the winter. Additionally, new gardens were added and old gardens expanded. Aging trees were replaced, in many cases with seedlings or cuttings from the original trees. (Left, courtesy of Hilary Forsyth.)

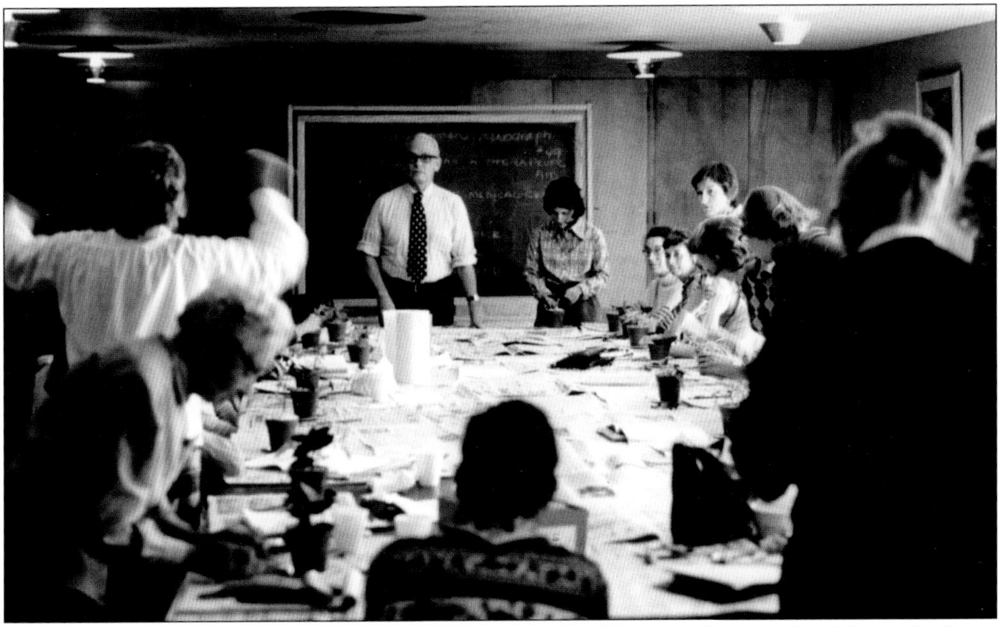

Horticultural Therapy Classes. Beginning in 1974, arboretum director Dr. Edward Duda, in association with program horticulturist Damon Olszowy, trained individuals to be horticultural therapists under a grant from the Connecticut Commission for Higher Education. Subsequent classes were supported by the US Department of Health, Education, and Welfare. Above, Howard Brooks, retired horticultural therapist from the Institute of Rehabilitation Medicine at New York University Medical Center, is shown conducting a workshop for individuals with physical challenges in 1978. Some of the training was performed at the Easter Seal Rehabilitation Center of Southwestern Connecticut in Stamford, including this session on forcing bulbs (below).

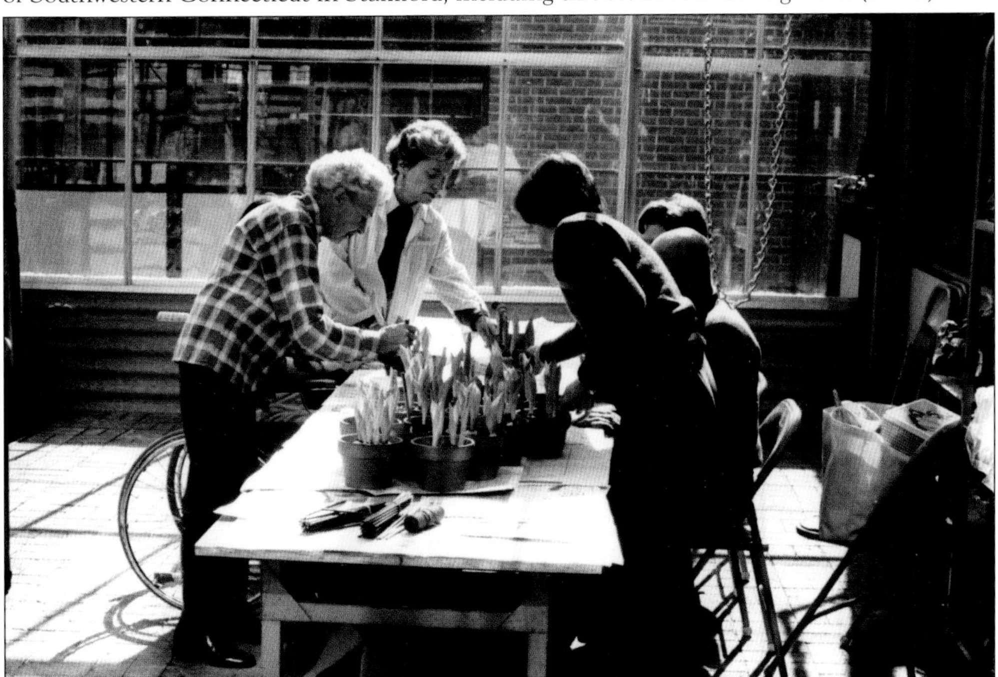

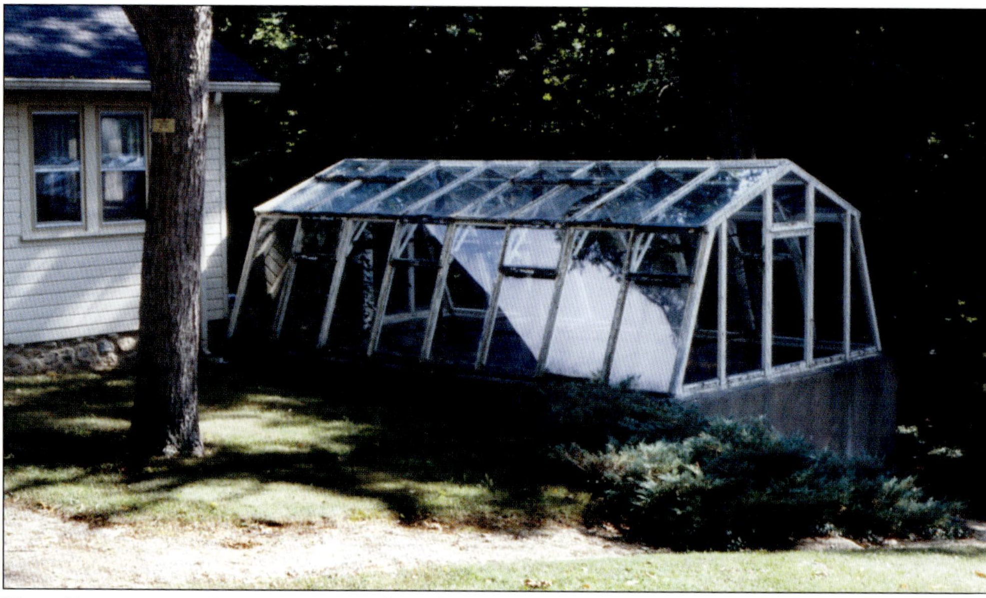

New Greenhouse Constructed. The arboretum's greenhouse near the Stone Laboratory was small and in disrepair (above). In the 1970s, the arboretum began the process of seeking donations for a new greenhouse building. In 1976, the arboretum received a 40-by-80-foot steel glasshouse structure as a donation from the Atlas Construction Company. The construction of the glasshouse had to wait until 1978 when the arboretum received a grant from the US Department of the Interior Bureau of Outdoor Recreation that, together with matching funds, permitted the arboretum to complete the construction and glaze the glass panels. The greenhouse is used for housing tropical plants and other exotic plants, such as cacti, as a teaching center for plant propagation, for demonstrations, and other plant exhibits. (Below, courtesy of Hannah Heyman.)

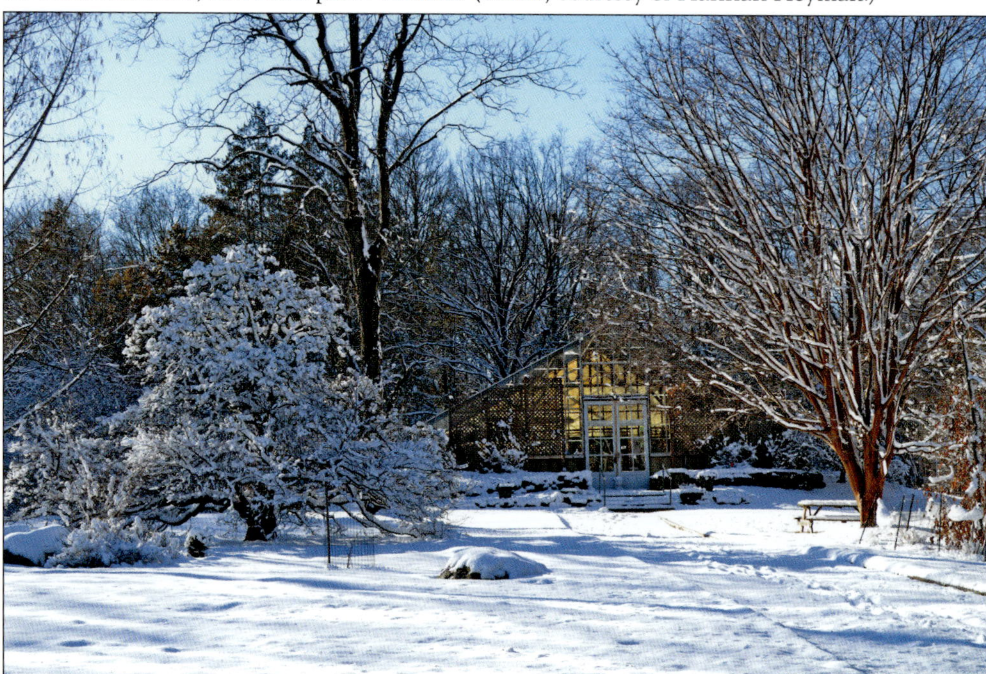

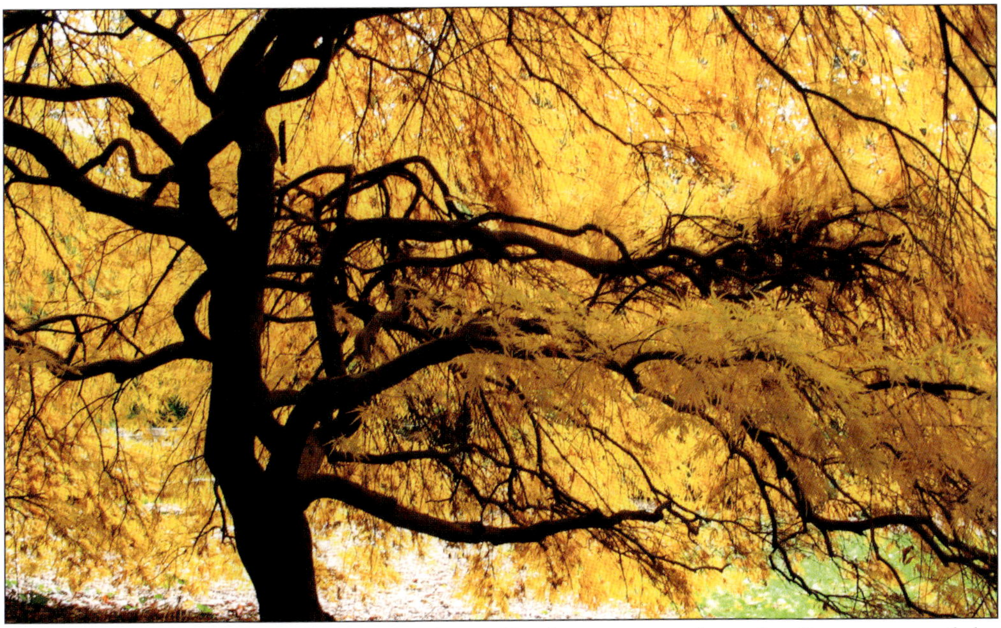

CONSTRUCTION OF THE MAINTENANCE SHED. Funds remaining from the Department of the Interior grant permitted the arboretum to construct a 30-by 84-foot storage and utility building near the greenhouse, not far from where the Yellow and Purple Gardens had once stood. At the arboretum, even a maintenance shed is beautified by its surroundings. This lovely Japanese maple (*Acer palmatum*) with yellow fall color grows in front of the shed.

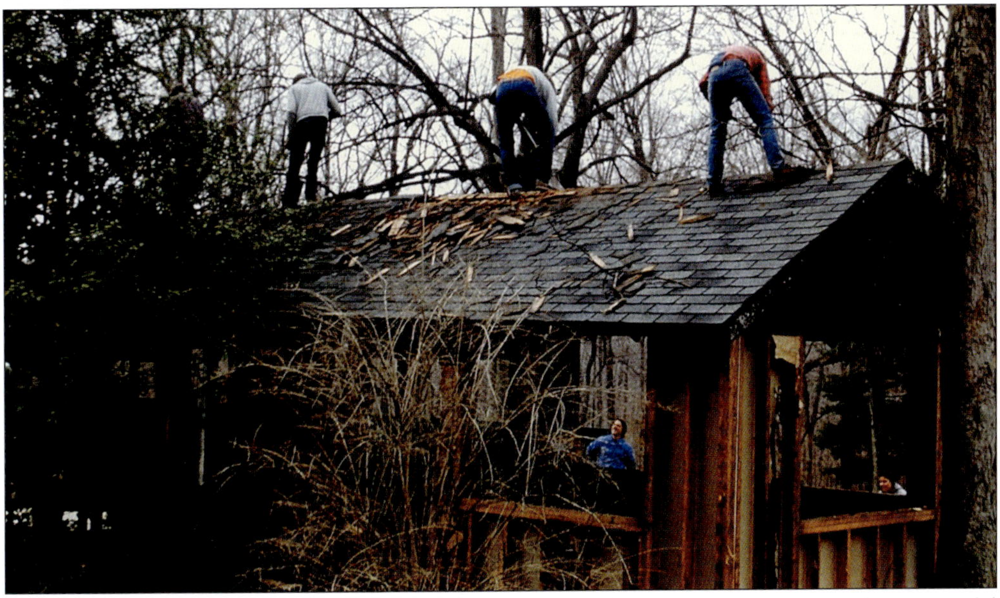

CHANGES MAKE WAY FOR THE FUTURE. Forsyth Lab and the insectary were no longer useful and were torn down in the late 1980s. Along with physical changes, arboretum oversight was changing. In 1994, the State Department of Environmental Protection surrendered title to the University of Connecticut's Stamford branch. A celebration presided over by Stamford mayor Stanley Esposito included introduction of the new director, Dr. Mark McDonnell, a University of Connecticut scientist studying the ecology of human populated areas.

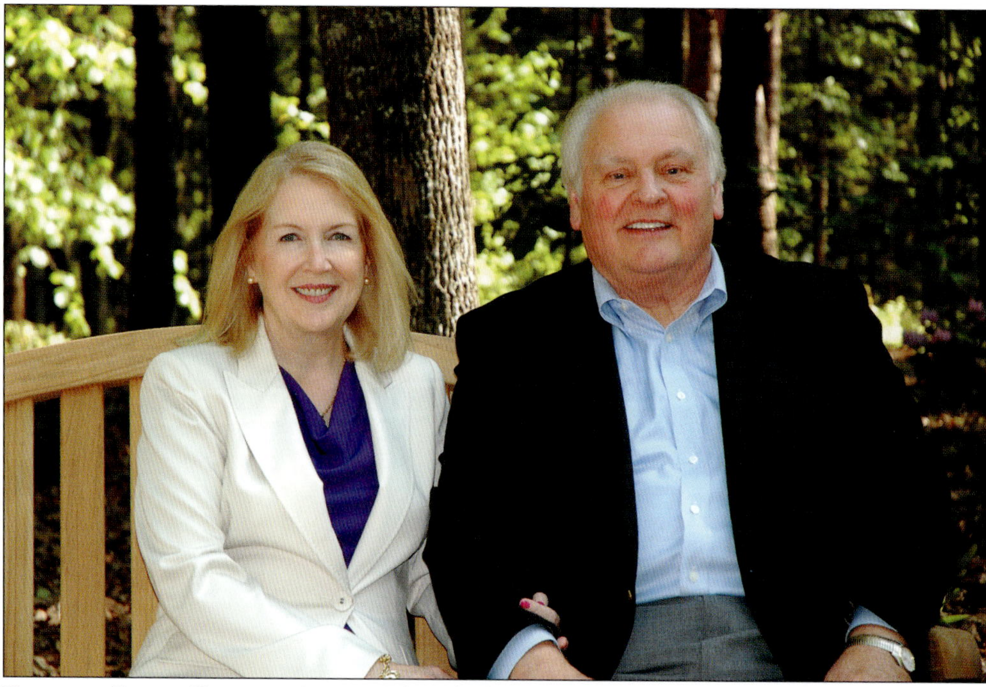

Bartlett Family Remains Active. Though the Bartlett family sold the property in 1965, they remain intertwined with the arboretum in many ways. Robert Sr.'s son, Robert Jr., entered the family business following in the footsteps of his father and grandfather. At the direction of the Bartlett family, the Stamford office of the F.A. Bartlett Tree Experts Company generously provides hundreds of hours of tree maintenance and care to the arboretum each year. Robert Jr. served as president of the Bartlett Arboretum Association, and his wife, Kate, has been an active volunteer over the years. F.A. Bartlett's daughter, Jane Bartlett Heisinger (below, seated at center), was a volunteer for many years, and a wildflower garden is named in her honor.

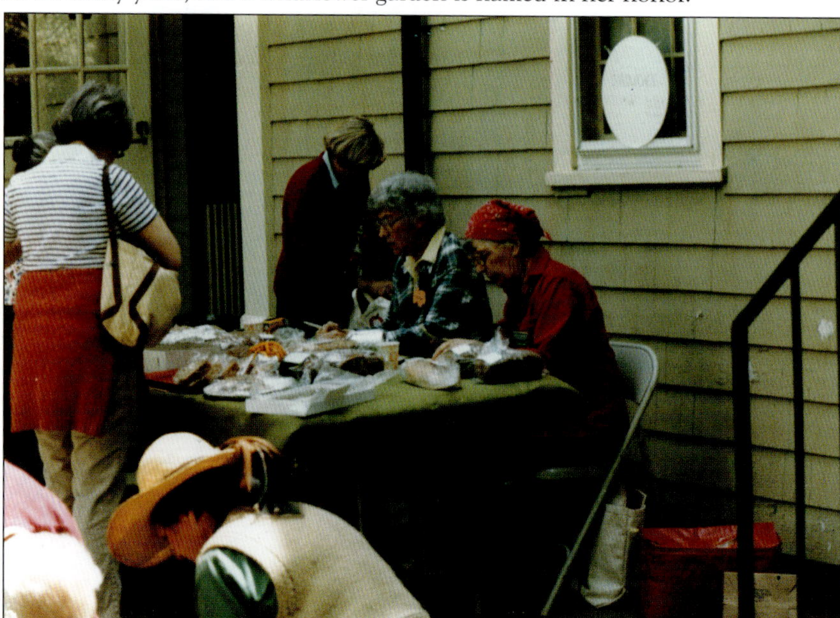

Three

Plant Collections and Gardens

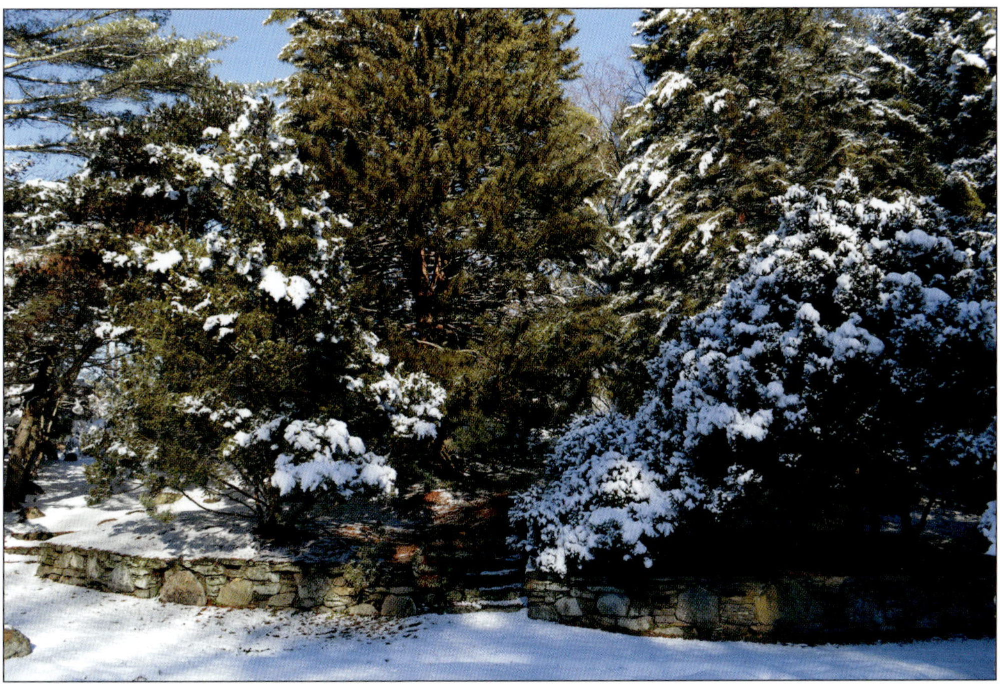

Conifer Garden Wall. One of the most picturesque collections in the arboretum is the Conifer Garden, and its stone wall is a work of art. Having withstood hurricanes, deer intrusion, and snowstorms, the wall must have been the focal point of the garden when the conifers were dwarf, but it recedes into the background today. Plant collections such as these are the backbone of an arboretum.

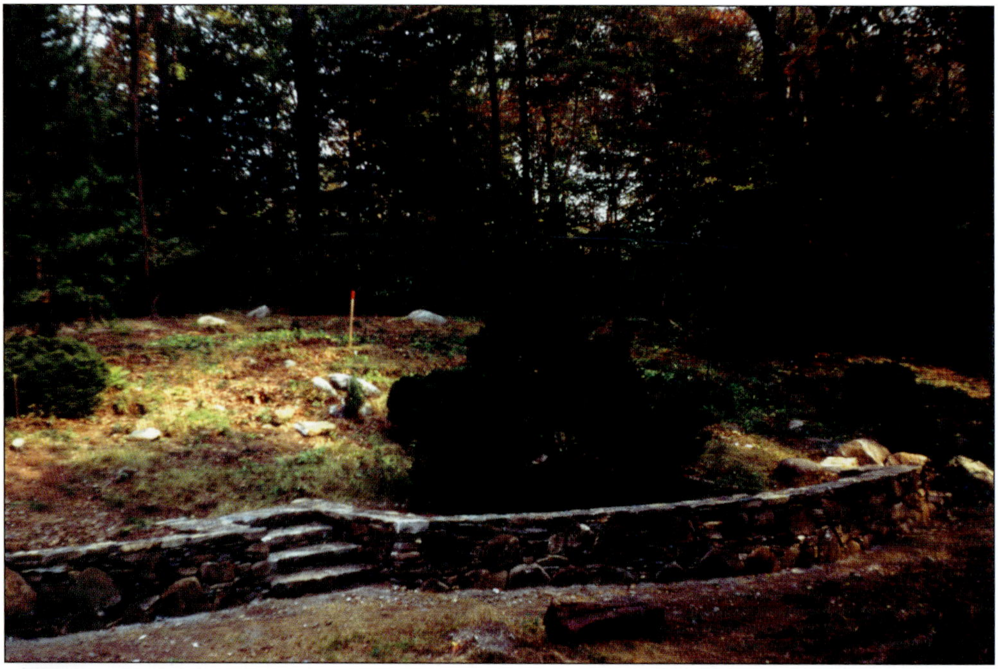

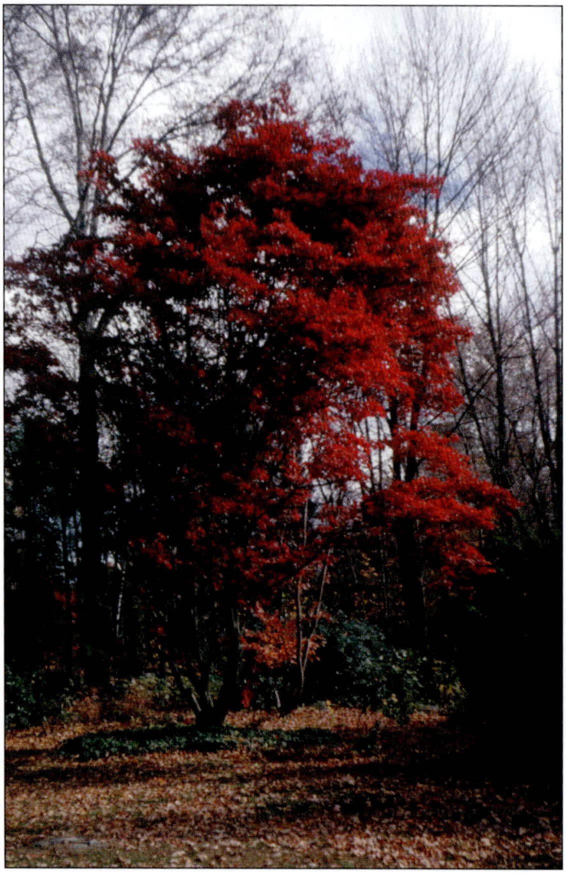

The Beginning of the Conifer Garden. Originally the site of F.A. Bartlett's plant nursery and his wife, Myrtle's, rock garden, the acre of land across from the Homestead was developed into a dwarf conifer garden beginning in 1969 after the transfer to the University of Connecticut. For years, it was the second-largest garden of its kind in the United States. Dr. Duda, director of the arboretum at the time, is credited with its original planting. Designed by the famous landscape architect A.E. Bye, it was intended to be a scientific reference garden, as well as a pleasingly aesthetic display of textures, colors, and growth patterns. It is home to two stately umbrella pines, as well as a *Cryptomeria* collection. Several junipers, pines, false cypresses, cypresses, spruces, hemlocks, arborvitae, firs, and yews make the backdrop for accents like Japanese maples (left), mountain laurel, oaks, and ash trees.

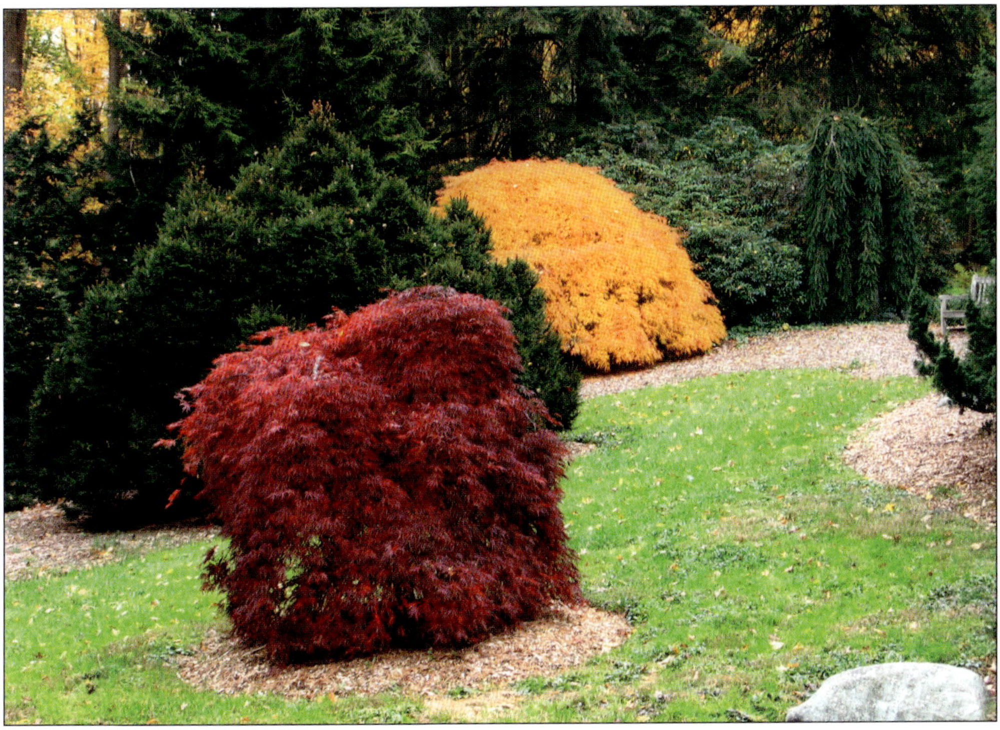

The Conifer Garden Grows. The original 250 plants comprising 150 species of dwarf conifers have culled themselves over the years, but the aesthetic intent is undiluted, even with the reduced number of plants. The architect used a synoptic arrangement, grouping plants of each genus together. The other striking point to note is that dwarfs do not stay small; while they grow very slowly, some as little as an inch in a year, the garden's plants are hardly small in stature some 50 years after they were first planted. Recently, the addition of two contiguous acres will allow for a rebirth of the dwarfs, as plans are under way to develop the new property. The juxtaposition of the fully grown dwarf conifers with the newly planted ones will create a remarkable contrast. It is hoped that it will become a reference garden for dwarf conifer connoisseurs the world over.

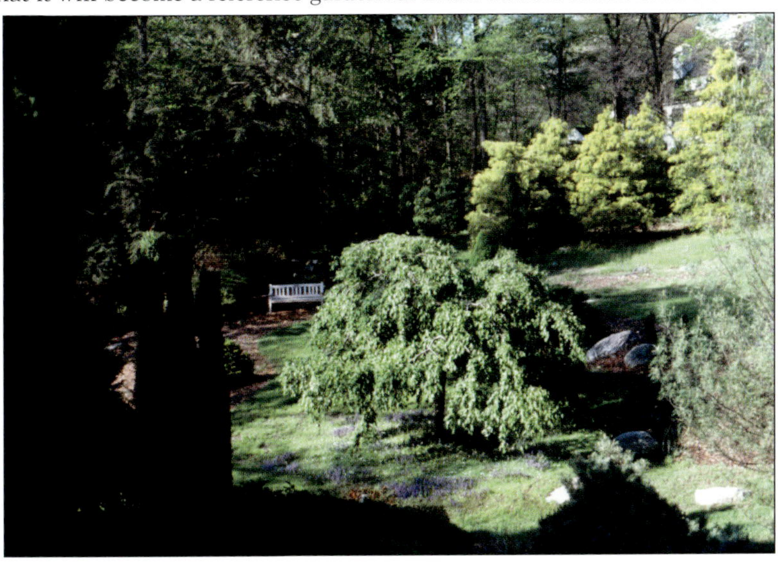

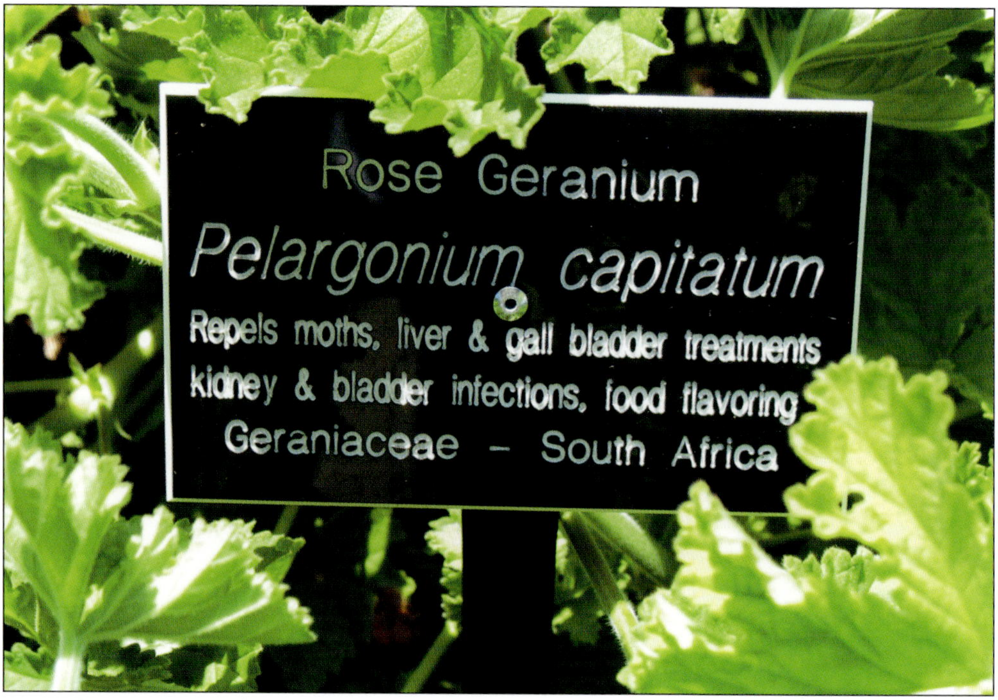

Herb Garden. Four classic quadrants charm the visitor with aromatic, culinary, medicinal, and economically interesting herbs. The plants are annual and perennial, native and tropical, flowering in all seasons with more than 100 species in a compact setting sure to delight the senses. Herbs are products people use every day in teas, medicines, and flavorings. The culinary section offers herbs like basil and French tarragon to flavor food. The aromatic section features fragrant herbs used in perfumes and essential oils. Applied correctly, the herbs in the medicinal section can treat indigestion, colds, and migraines. Food additives, dyes, and fibers are featured in the economic quadrant.

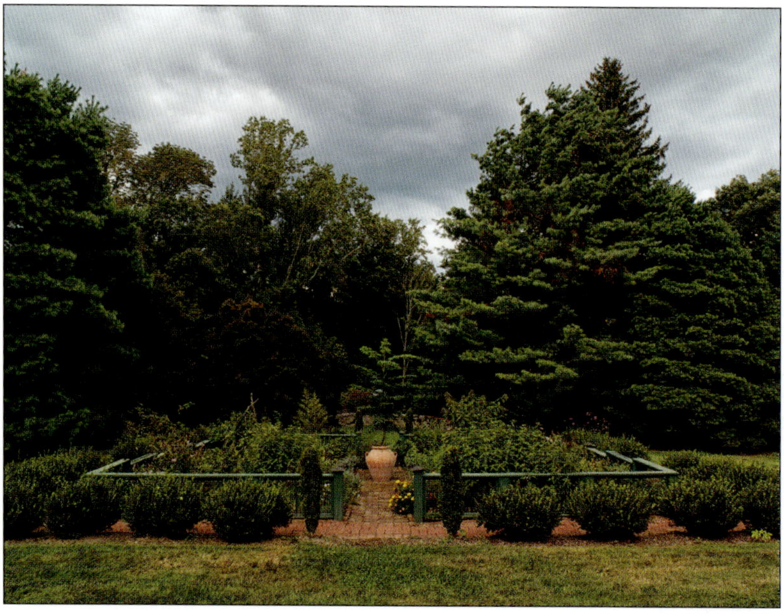

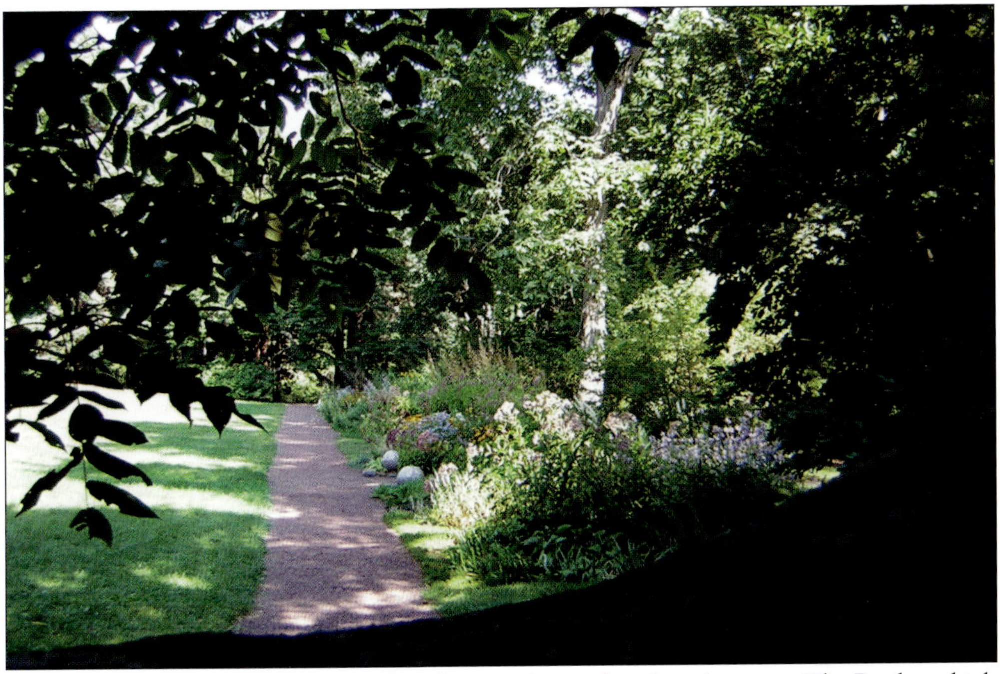

Perennial Border. Three perennial gardens are featured at the arboretum. The Border, which began in the 1970s as an iris display garden by the Iris Society in Stamford, is 140 feet long and approximately 14 feet wide. In the early 1980s, it started to evolve under the directorship of Ted Lockwood (who served in the position from 1979 to 1987) as tired bulbs were replaced with colorful perennials. Today, it is packed with more than 100 varieties of plants, paying close attention to natives and a shady/sunny mix depending on where they are situated in the garden. The garden attracts pollinators and is a source of nourishment or a host for their eggs. It is designated as a Monarch Waystation. The Border takes care of itself, with only a weekly weeding and infrequent watering. High maintenance plants are avoided. Meticulous attention is paid to the arrangement of color and texture, so that every season offers a different visual tapestry.

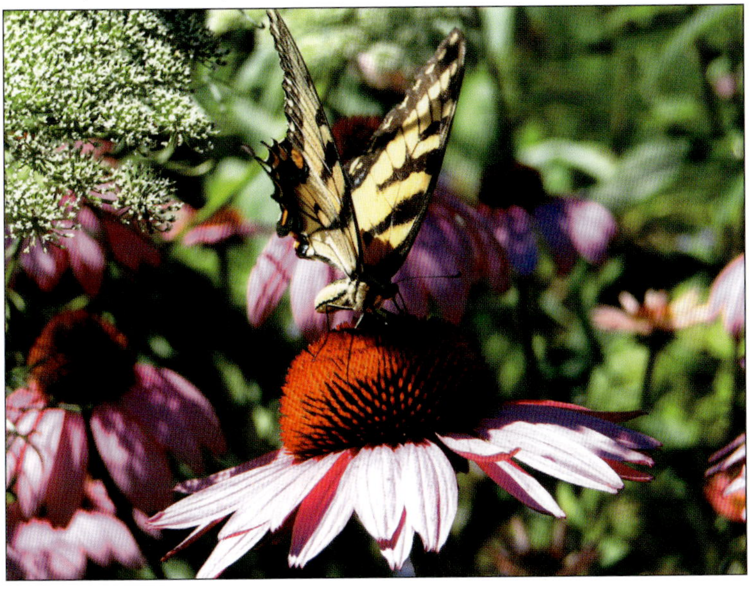

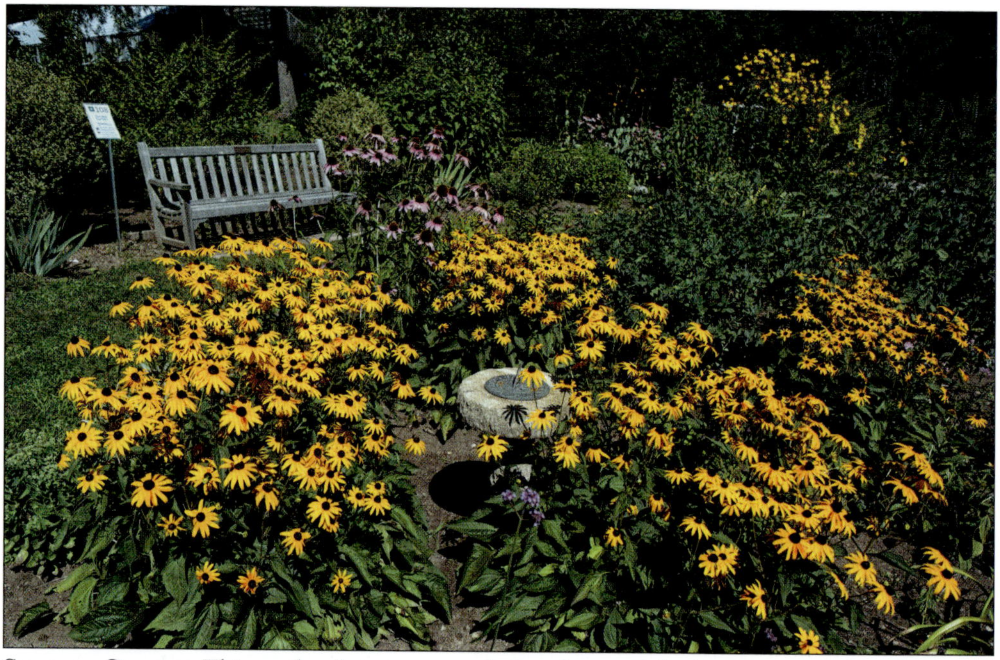

Sundial Garden. This garden features a sundial and one of the best vistas of the arboretum. It has full-sun exposure, so all the plants in the garden can be considered drought tolerant and fairly deer resistant. Many of the plants have been chosen to attract birds, butterflies, and bees in the area. (Courtesy of Dan Lenore.)

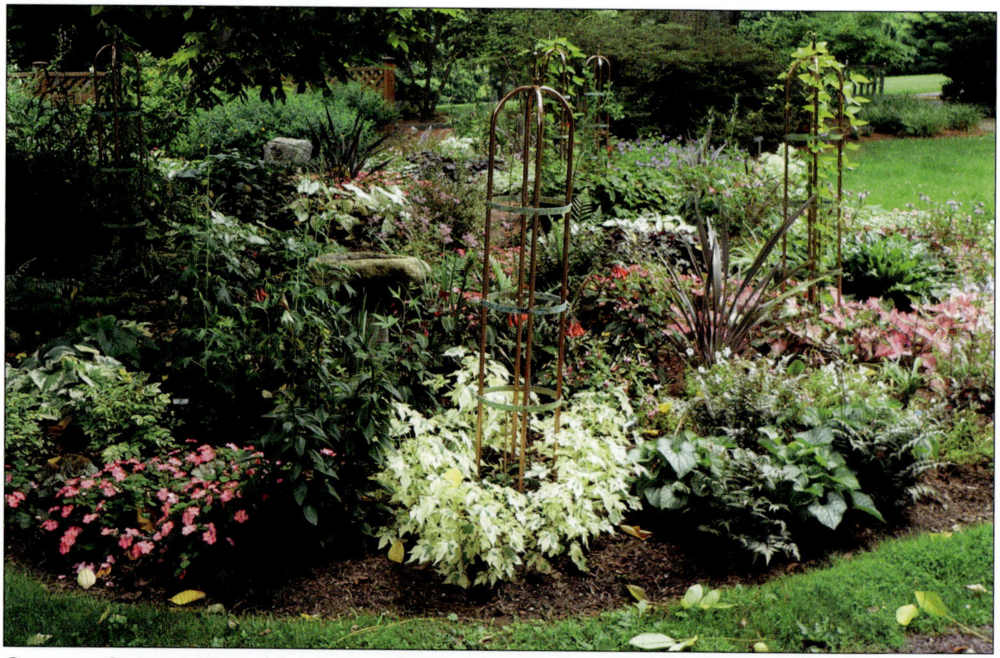

Cottage Garden. Named for the popular British gardens in the 18th century, the Cottage Garden sat behind a cottage built in 1934, which was destroyed during Hurricane Sandy in 2014. The garden plants enjoy both sun and shade, beginning in spring with the hellebores (*Helleborus* spp.) and finishing the growing season with a display of Japanese toad lilies (*Tricyrtis hirta*) and chrysanthemums.

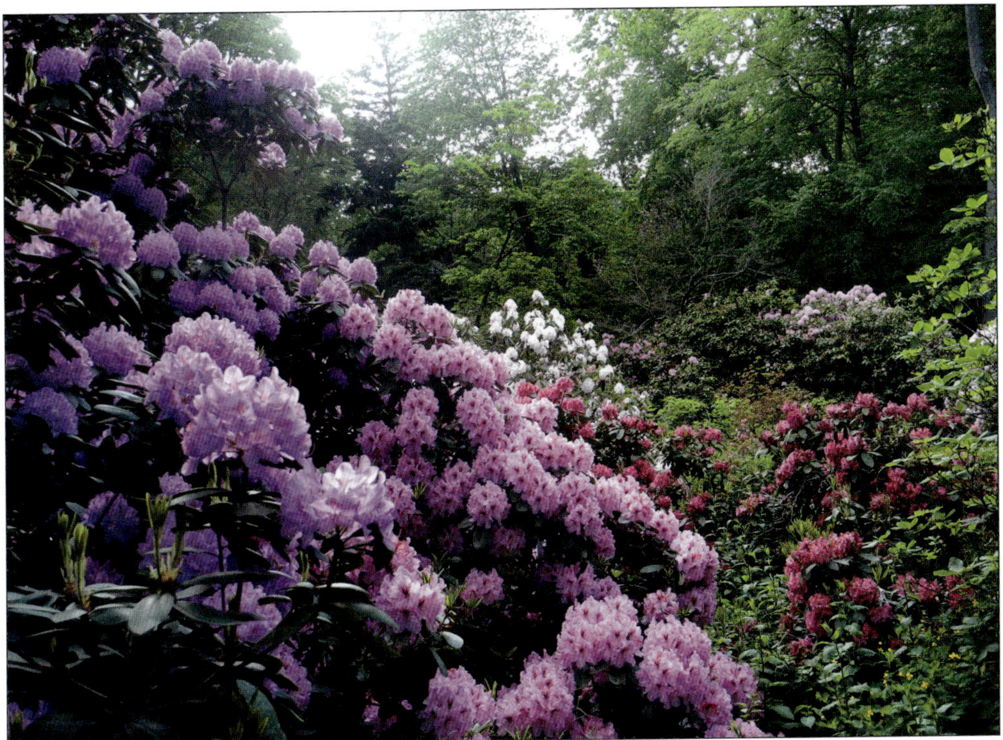

Mehlquist Garden. In 1966, the so-called ericaceous area no. 1 was established by Dr. Gustav Mehlquist, a noted plant breeder at the University of Connecticut. He developed a rough map for the records of several hundred plants in 15 sections defined by a system of paths. Since this inauspicious beginning, several employees and volunteers have taken on the task to map and remap the garden, which was dedicated to Dr. Mehlquist years later. He is credited with developing hardy, high-quality rhododendrons and azaleas, but the garden is also home to highbush blueberries, Japanese andromeda, *Enkianthus*, and mountain laurel, the Connecticut state flower, under a canopy of several hardwood trees.

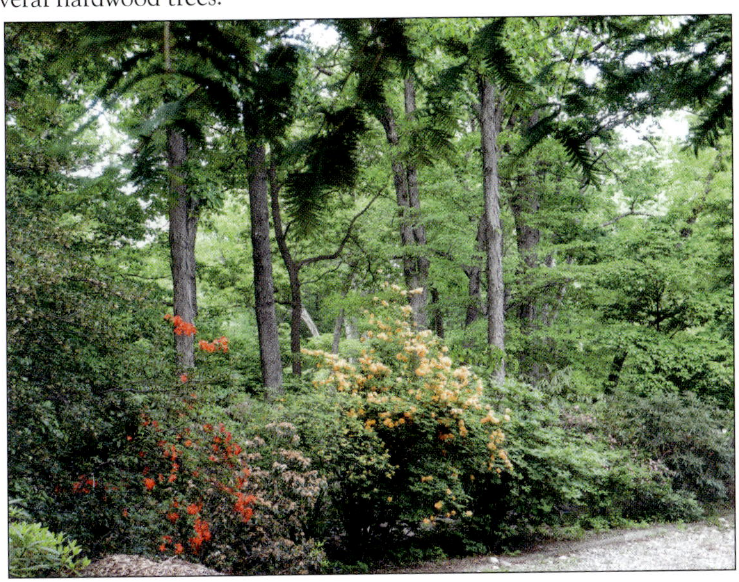

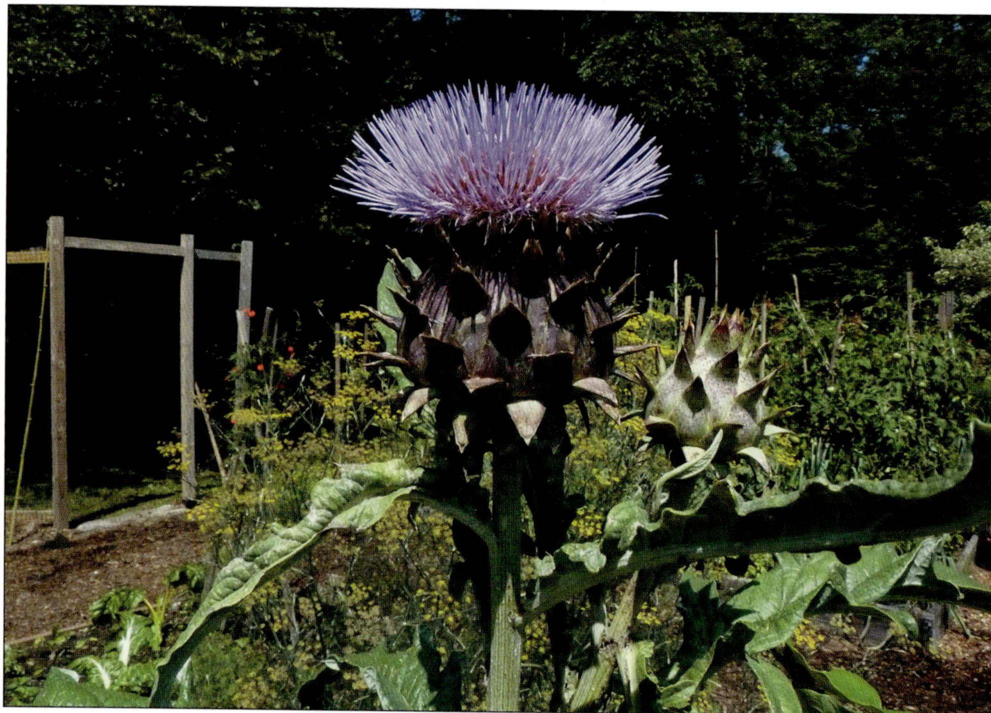

VEGETABLE GARDEN. When the Bartlett family lived on the property, this sunny walled-in garden was the site of many lively parties. In 2008, a vegetable garden was established on this site with decoratively arranged raised garden beds, pathways, ornaments, espaliered fruit trees, fruiting shrubs, and a variety of vegetables, both perennial and seasonal. The garden is completely organic, with directly sown seeds as well as sets planted in the spring. Natural amendments such as egg shells, banana peels, and seaweed are used to encourage growth, and insects are deterred with companion plants such as garlic, onions, and marigolds. Many flowers are grown to attract pollinators and beneficial insects. (Above, courtesy of Elaine Hjelte; below, courtesy of Dan Lenore.)

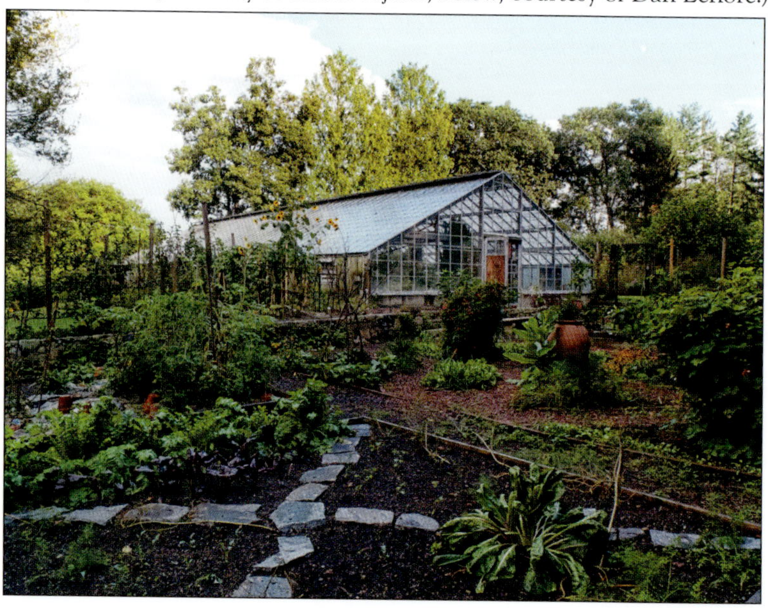

Woodland Treasures/Jane Heisinger Memorial Wild Flower Garden. Filled with more than 100 local species on about one quarter of an acre, this garden represents the diversity of attractive native plants that can be used for the home landscape. A section originally known as the Jane B. Heisinger Memorial Wild Flower Garden (planted in 1992 by Joan Faust, Carol Levine, Lovel Perkins, Edie Reiman, and Alice Smith) has been undergoing renovation. It was established as a living memorial to Francis Bartlett's daughter, Jane B. Heisinger (below, right), who died in 1991. The Woodland Treasures area emphasizes that native plants are important to the local ecosystem because they provide sustenance and habitat for native insects, bees, butterflies, birds, and animals. Some of the noted plants in this garden are Virginia bluebells (*Mertensia virginica*), trout lilies (*Erythronium americanum*), mayapples (*Podophyllum peltatum*), black cohosh (*Actaea racemosa*, right), and jack-in-the-pulpit (*Arisaema triphyllum*).

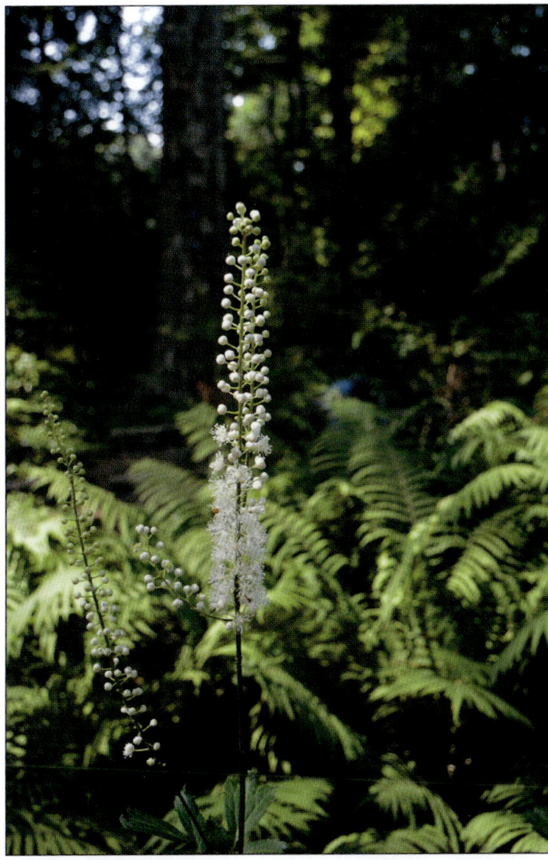

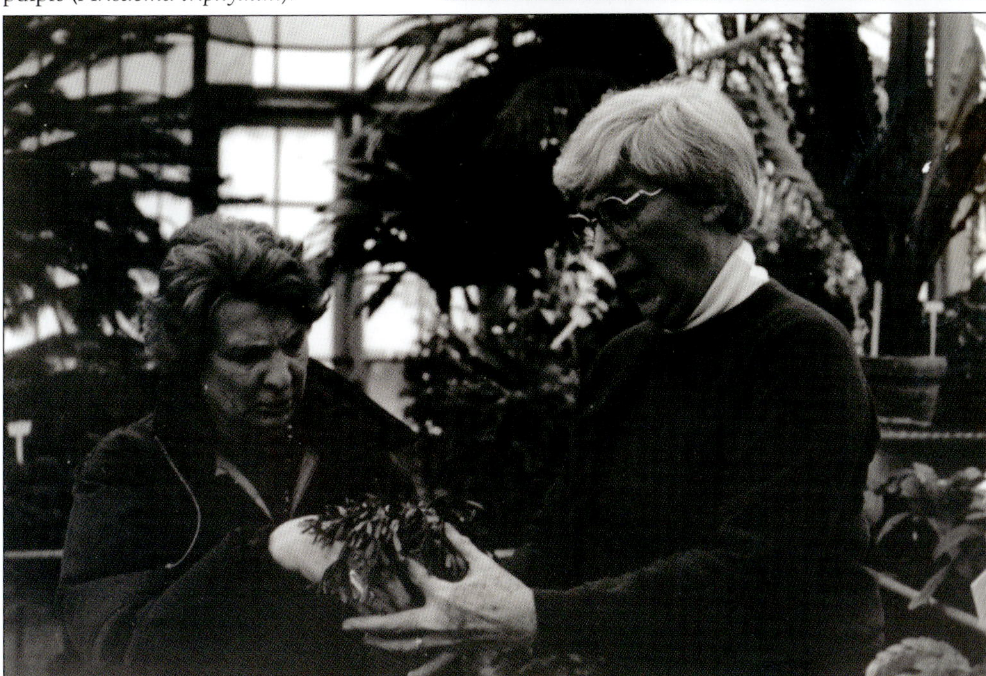

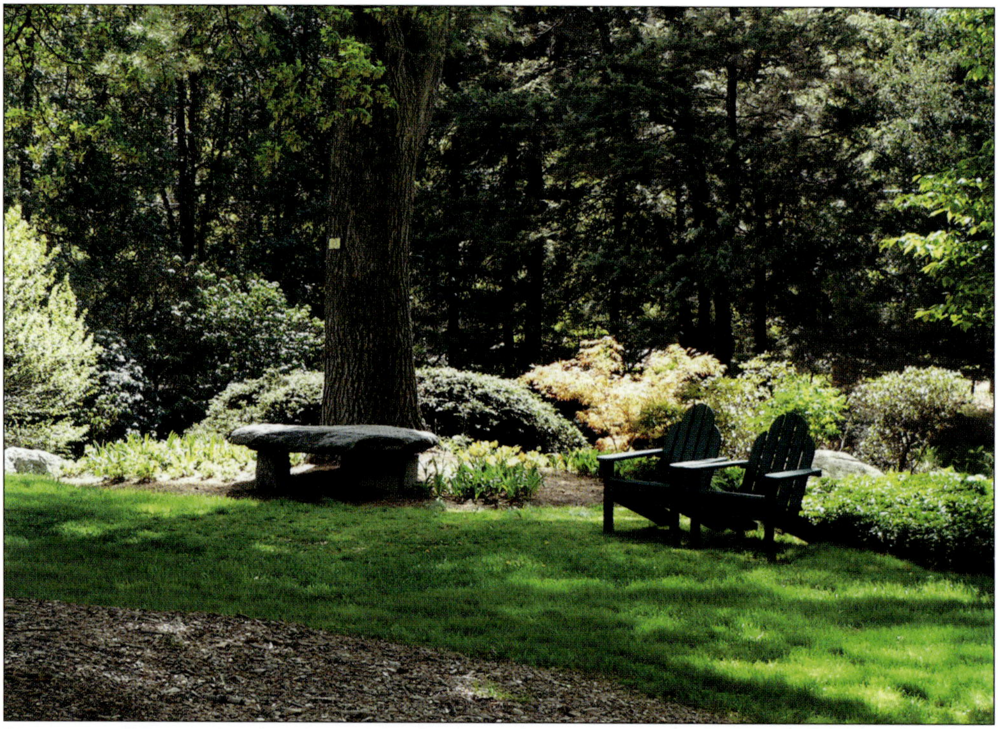

Secluded Garden. In the spring of 1980, twelve students from the Horticulture Club at the University of Connecticut volunteered to transform a corner of the arboretum into the Secluded Garden. Over two days, they planted 100 shrubs according to the university's landscape architect John Alexopoulos's plan. They mounded wet areas and planted them with azaleas and rhododendrons around the perimeter of the mounds to create a sort of enclosure. Additionally, they planted daylilies and other perennials, and annuals were added later for more color. Over the years, the garden has evolved into a lovely area filled with perennial plants and shrubs that put on a show throughout the season.

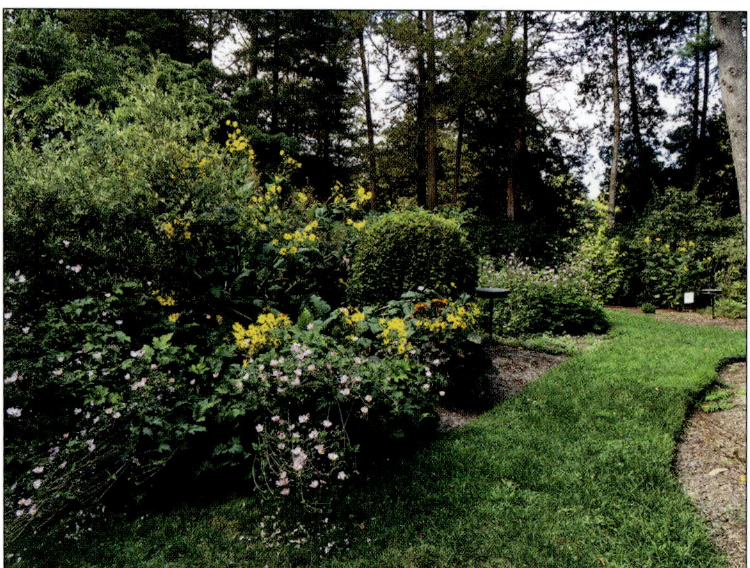

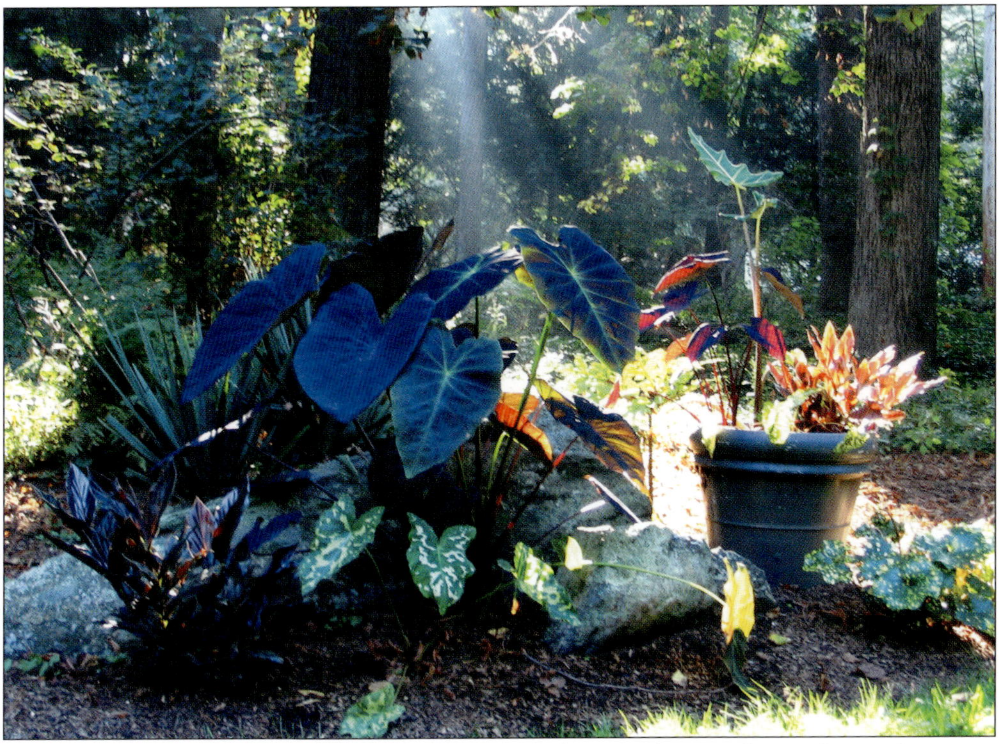

Tropical Garden. The tropical garden vacations indoors in the greenhouse during the winter months, and some of the plants are moved to an area adjacent to the Secluded Garden during the growing season. Lulos (*Solanum quitoense*) and tamarillos (*Solanum betaceum*), a South American fruit related to the tomato, are among the exotic favorites in the garden. Bananas (*Musa* spp.) dominate the garden and will even produce small bunches of fruit, albeit unripened during the short growing season. Another favorite for its finely tufted leaves and graceful habit is the papyrus (*Cyperus papyrus*), a giant species of sedge native to marsh edges. Lynette Farinas generously donated the tropical garden in memory of her husband.

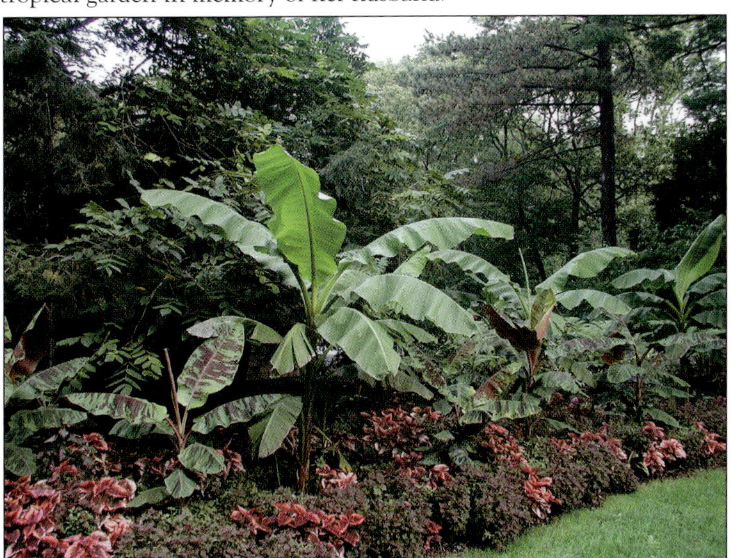

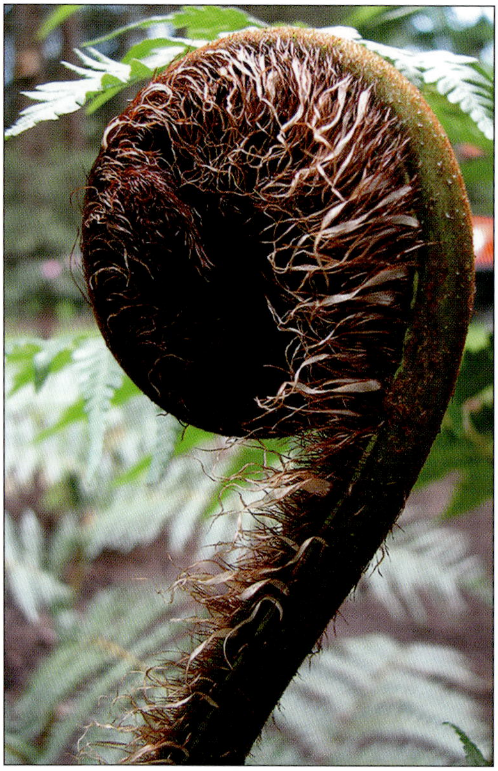

FERN ALLÉE. This pathway is bordered on each side by more than 60 varieties of ferns, which thrive with other shade-loving plants. The woodlands and wetlands of the arboretum are speckled with at least 22 varieties of native ferns. Since they were far from accessible trails, this special area was created to showcase nonnatives alongside natives. As ferns are unfolding their fronds, they are known as fiddleheads. Ferns are among the oldest plant forms, dating back as much as 350 million years. The arboretum's collection includes the tatting fern (*Athyrium filix-femina* 'Frizelliae'), the Christmas fern (*Polystichum acrostichoides*), and the upside-down fern (*Arachnoides standishii*), among others.

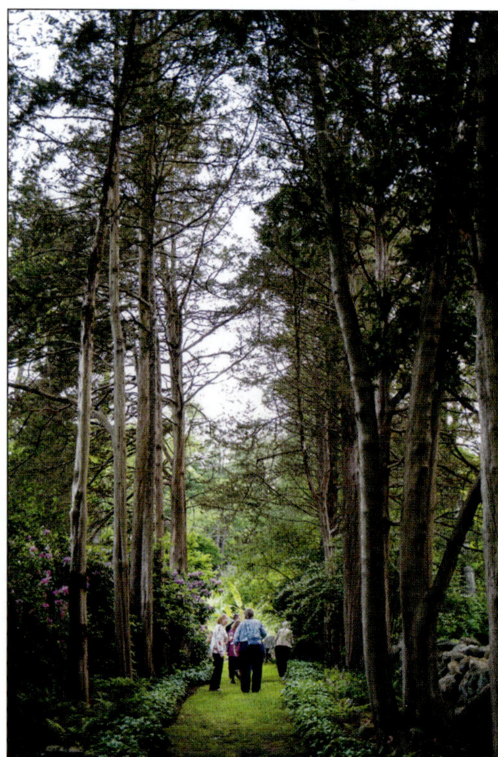

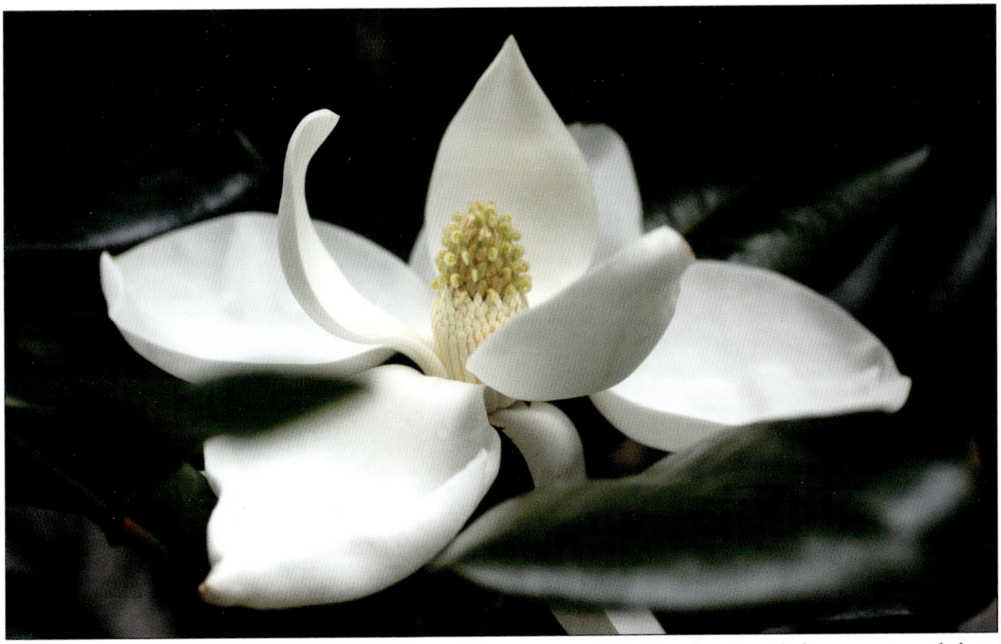

Kate and Robert Bartlett Jr. Magnolia Collection. The Bartlett family has continued their interest in the arboretum and their contributions to the collections established by F.A. Bartlett more than 100 years ago. One of the early plantings was southern magnolia (M. *grandiflora*, above), which Bartlett planted on the side of the Homestead. It had giant white flowers and evergreen leaves. It suffered damage, probably due to marginal hardiness, and was removed in 1979. Robert Bartlett Jr. has a keen interest in magnolias and has provided the arboretum with several new hybrids in recent years. The collection has grown to more than 40 cultivars of magnificent star magnolias (M. *stellata*), Chinese magnolias (M. *sinensis*), and saucer magnolias (M. x *soulangeana*, below), including this one called "Pinkie."

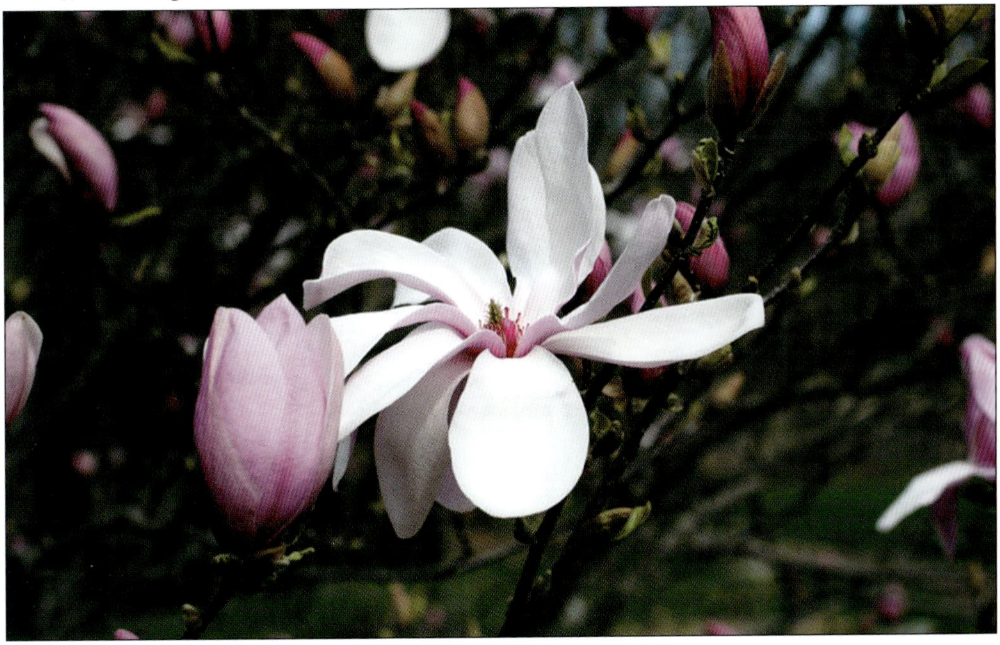

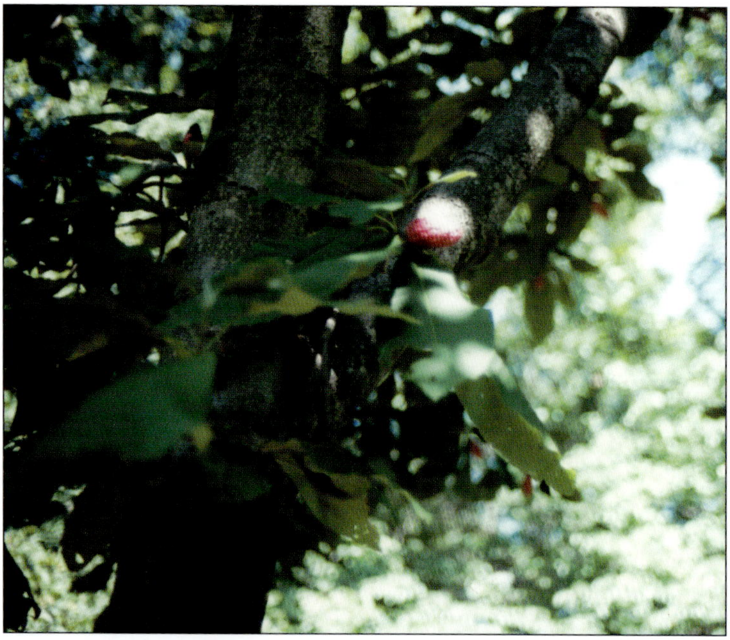

UMBRELLA MAGNOLIA. The umbrella magnolia (*Magnolia tripetala*) is a 40-foot native tree with an open habit named for its leaves, which are tufted at the tips, giving the impression of small umbrellas. Huge white flowers appear after the leaves in spring and are followed by long bunches of reddish fruit.

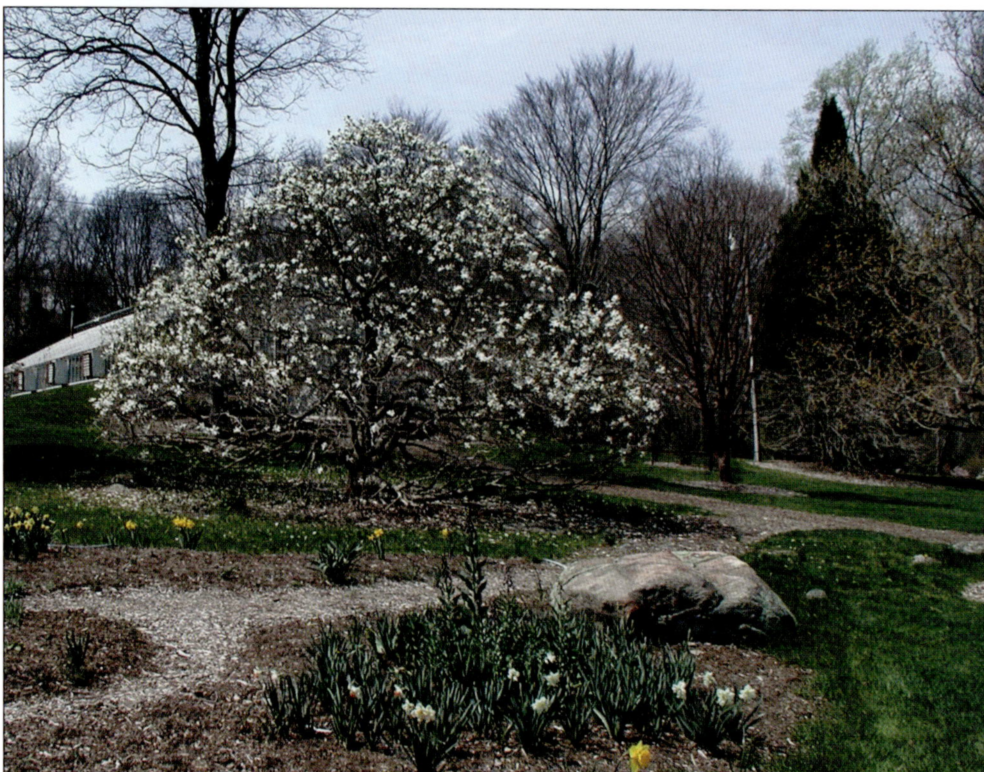

STAR MAGNOLIA (MAGNOLIA STELLATA). More a large shrub than a tree, star magnolia produces flowers before the leaves, making it a true harbinger of spring. Multi-petaled white flowers on the arboretum's beauty, the cultivar 'Centennial,' are tinged with pink on the edges. It is an attractive plant in all seasons with its fuzzy buds and silvery bark in winter.

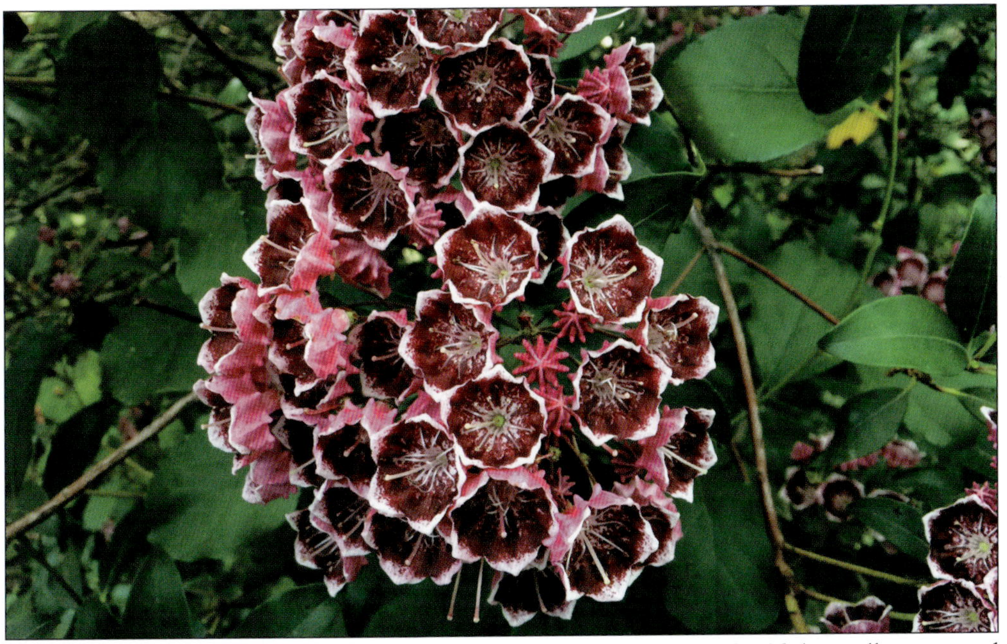

Laurel Collection. Connecticut's state flower, mountain laurel (*Kalmia latifolia*), is well represented at the arboretum with as many as 150 different forms of the plant on the grounds dating back to 1971. Two other natives thrive as well: sheep laurel (*K. angustifolia*) and eastern bog laurel (*K. polifolia*). They can be found in the Conifer Garden and around the main house. Native laurels have white to pink flowers and broadleaf evergreen leaves. Mountain laurel can get very large when grown in the right conditions, while sheep laurel remains low-growing (one to three feet). Bog laurel is a very small plant, barely reaching two feet, with hot pink flowers, and can be found growing near wet areas. Many of the arboretum specimens were donated by Dr. R.A. Jaynes, former plant geneticist at the Connecticut Agricultural Experiment Station in New Haven.

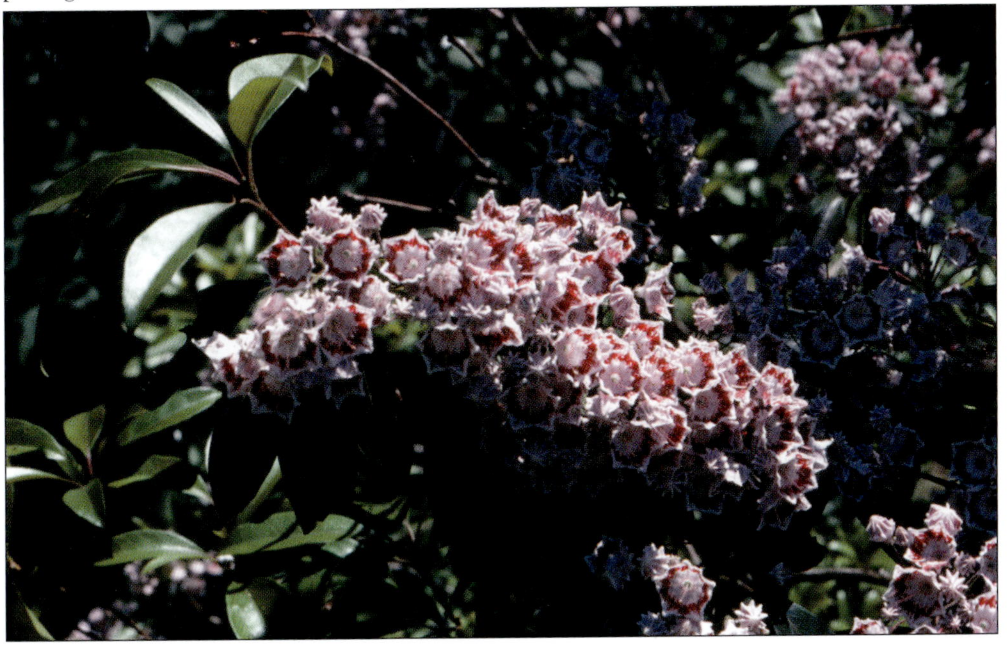

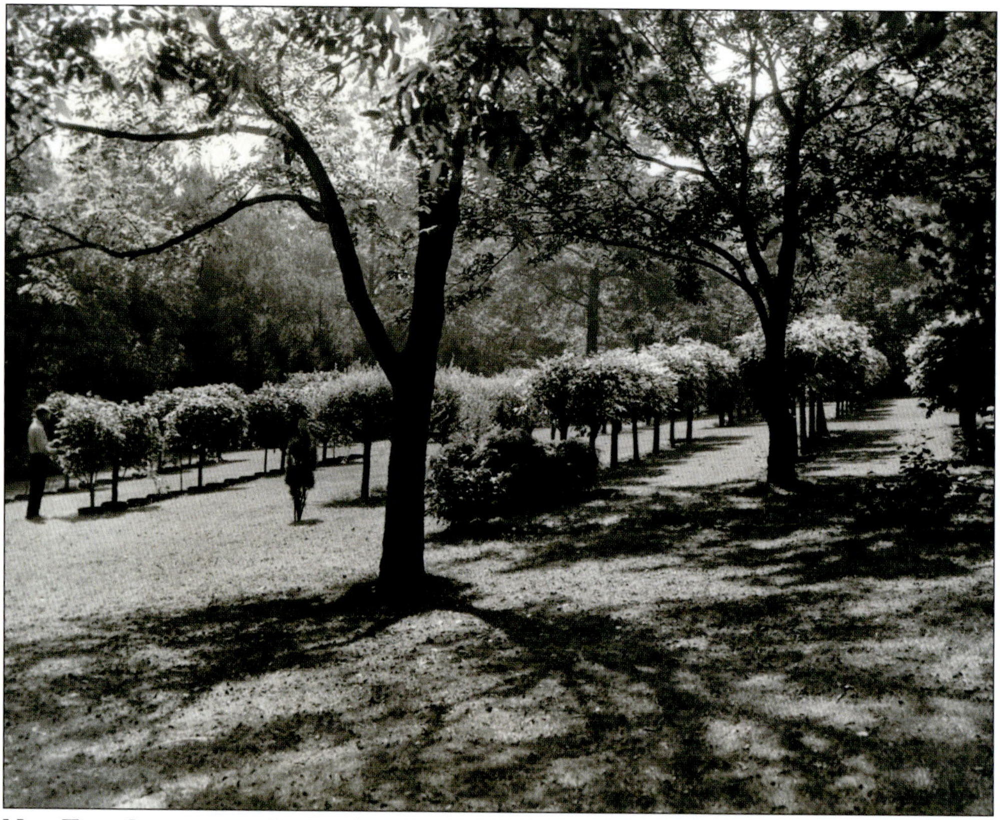

Nut Tree Collection. Dr. Bartlett was especially enamored of nut trees, and several of his plantings remain to this day. Pecans, walnuts, butternuts, the heartnut, and horse chestnuts are scattered about the property. In the foreground is a black walnut (*Juglans nigra*) guarding the pollarded trees.

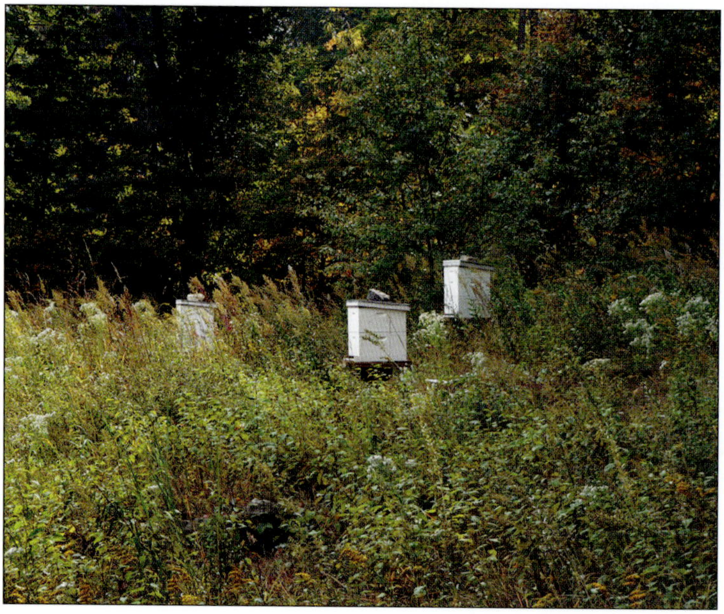

The Danoff Bruder Family Garden (Meadow). The arboretum began an effort in 2000 to clear a flat area near its High Ridge Road border to create a natural meadow of grasses and wildflowers. It was dedicated to the Danoff Bruder family in memory of deceased family members. The arboretum established several beehives in the meadow, and honey is a much sought-after product sold at the arboretum each fall.

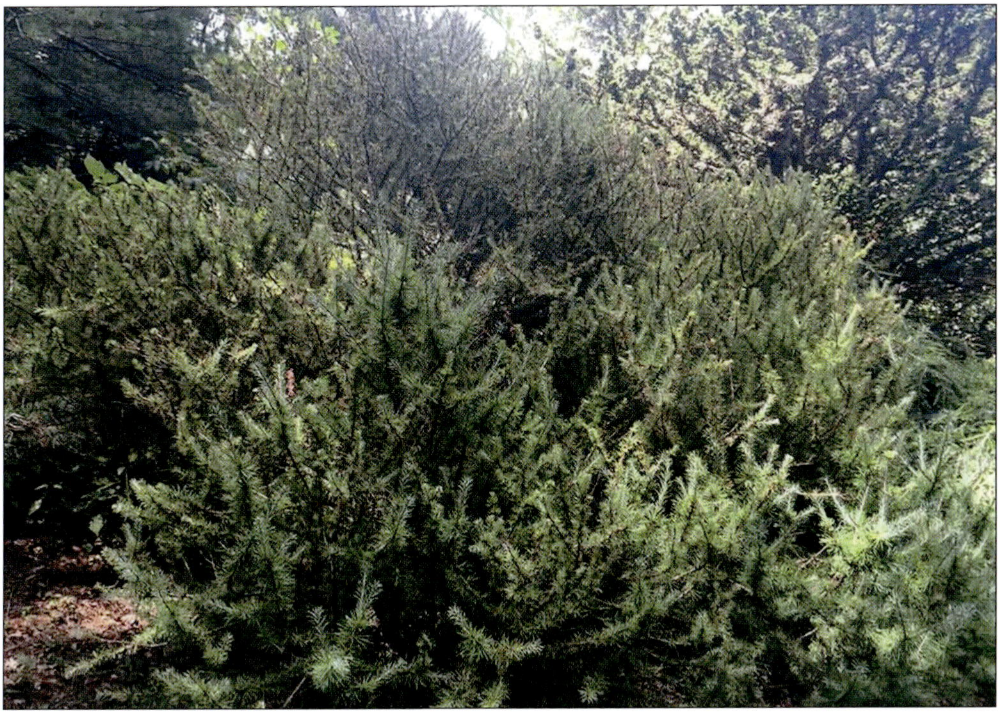

Witches'-Broom Collection. A witches'-broom is a characteristic of some coniferous evergreens. It is an abnormal growth of dense, darker green foliage near the inner truncated branches that mound into a form similar to representations of witches' brooms. They can be created by a natural mutation or by a parasite or virus that causes the natural growth to mutate. Dr. Sidney Waxman, a noted University of Connecticut horticulturist who studied this, developed several varieties from seedlings and donated 12 of them in the early 1980s, adding to a small collection already at the arboretum. His donated brooms were all mutants of white pine (*Pinus strobus*).

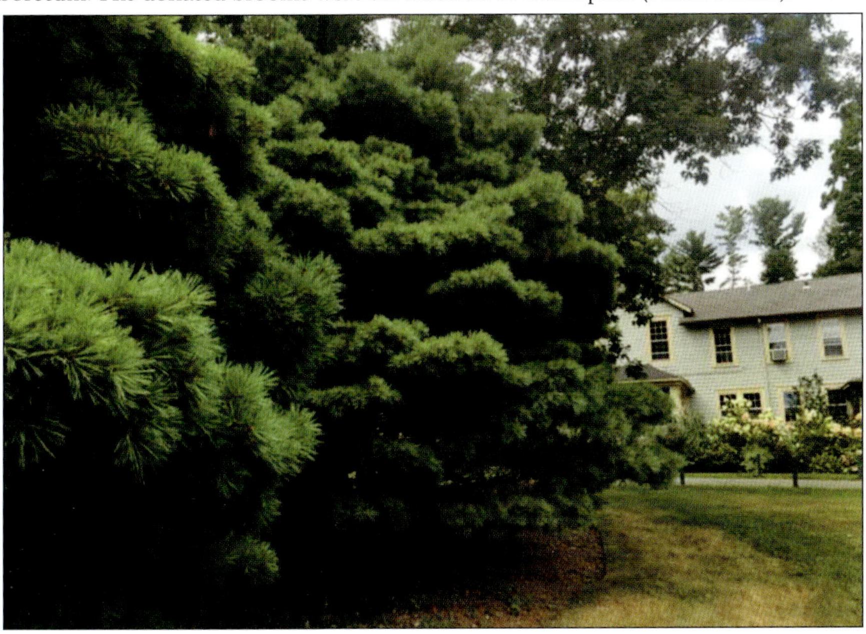

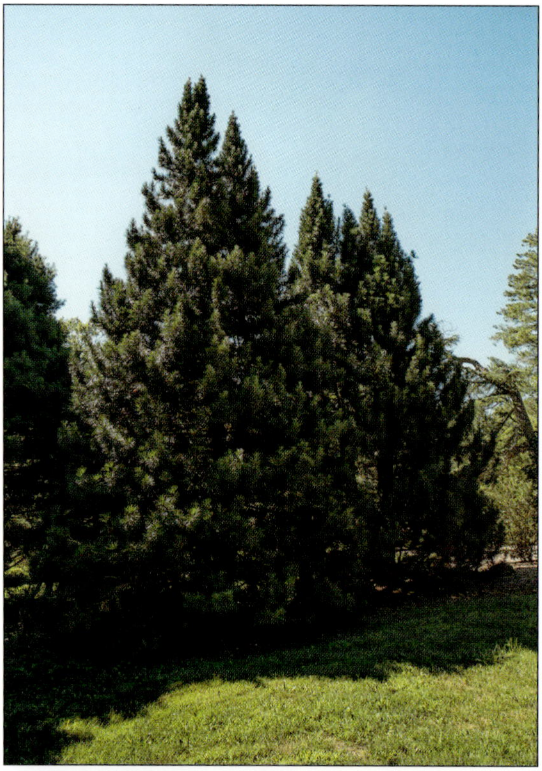

Pinetum. A large grouping of needled evergreens, including pines, spruces, true cedars, false cypress, and hemlocks, is clustered near the edge of the cultivated grounds and is known as the Pinetum. Among the more magnificent specimens originally found there is the cedar of Lebanon (*Cedrus libani*), a grand tree with broad branching and a thick trunk. In recent years, it has been damaged by storms and is overshadowed by the Japanese umbrella pines (*Sciadopitys verticillata*, left), with needles that diverge around the stem giving it an umbrella effect, and weeping hemlock (*Tsuga canadensis* 'Pendula,' at left below), which is a splendid example of a graceful pendulous conifer. (Left, courtesy of Dan Lenore.)

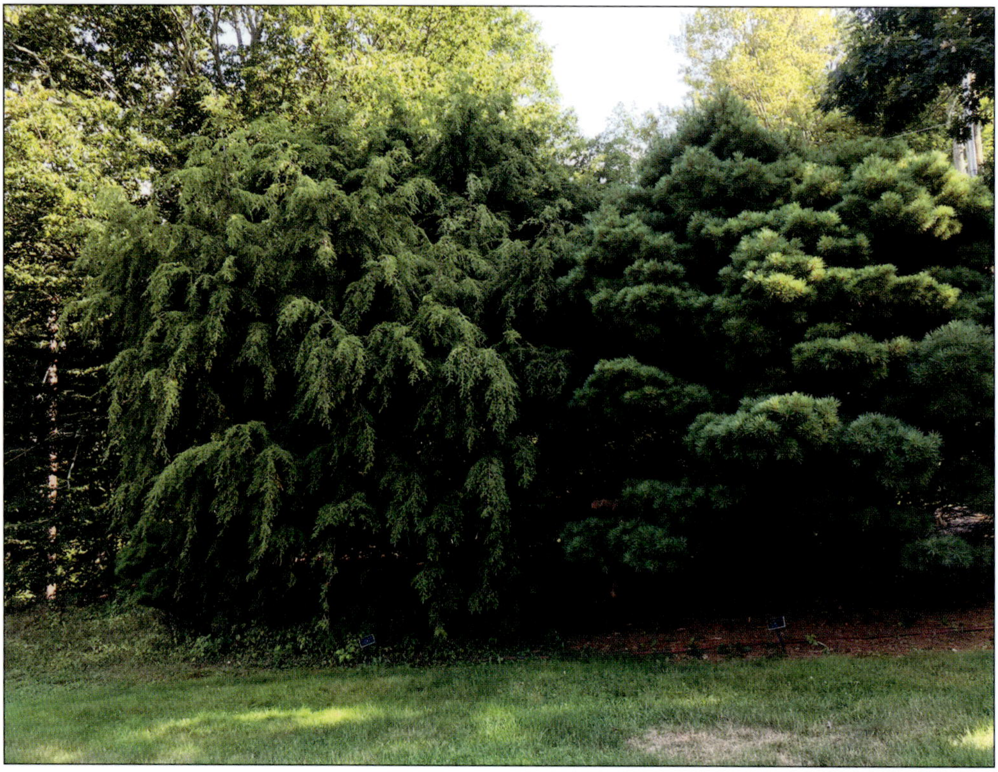

CACTUS AND SUCCULENTS. The original collection of cactus and succulents was inherited from the University of Connecticut. Over the years, cuttings were donated from the New York Botanical Garden, and gifts of seeds and plants were added, increasing the collection to as many as 140 species. In the 1980s, the collection thrived under the care of volunteer Bill Dockendorf. The collection of succulents and cacti has familiar specimens from the Americas such as the prickly pear (*Opuntia* spp., at right, lower left), as well as more exotic specimens like green stick (*Euphorbia tirucalli*) from east Africa and living stones (*Lithops* spp.), native to southwest Africa. (Right, courtesy of Dan Lenore.)

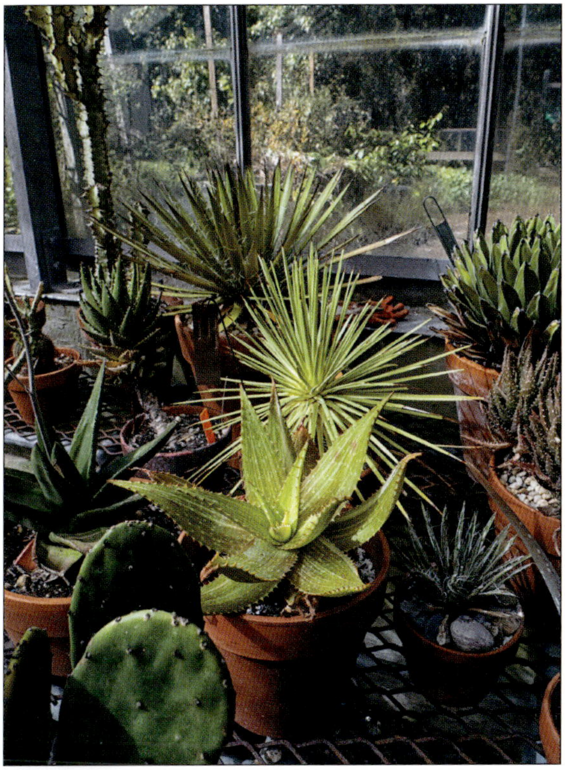

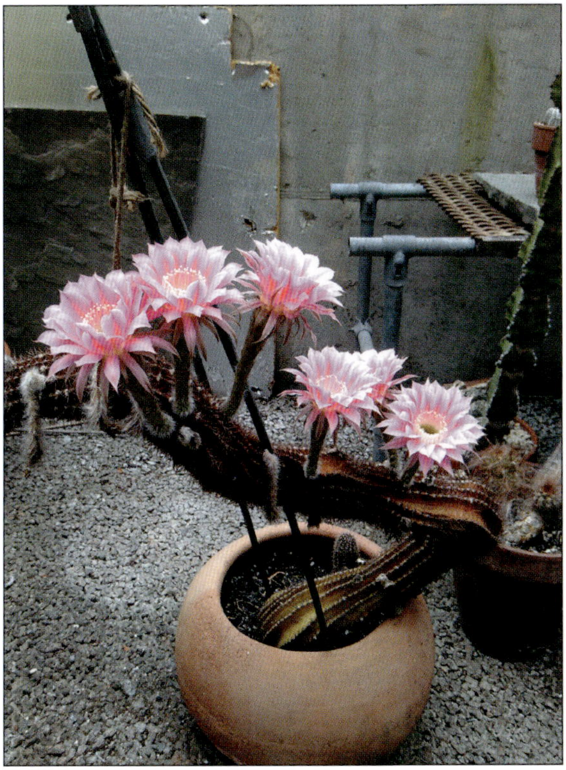

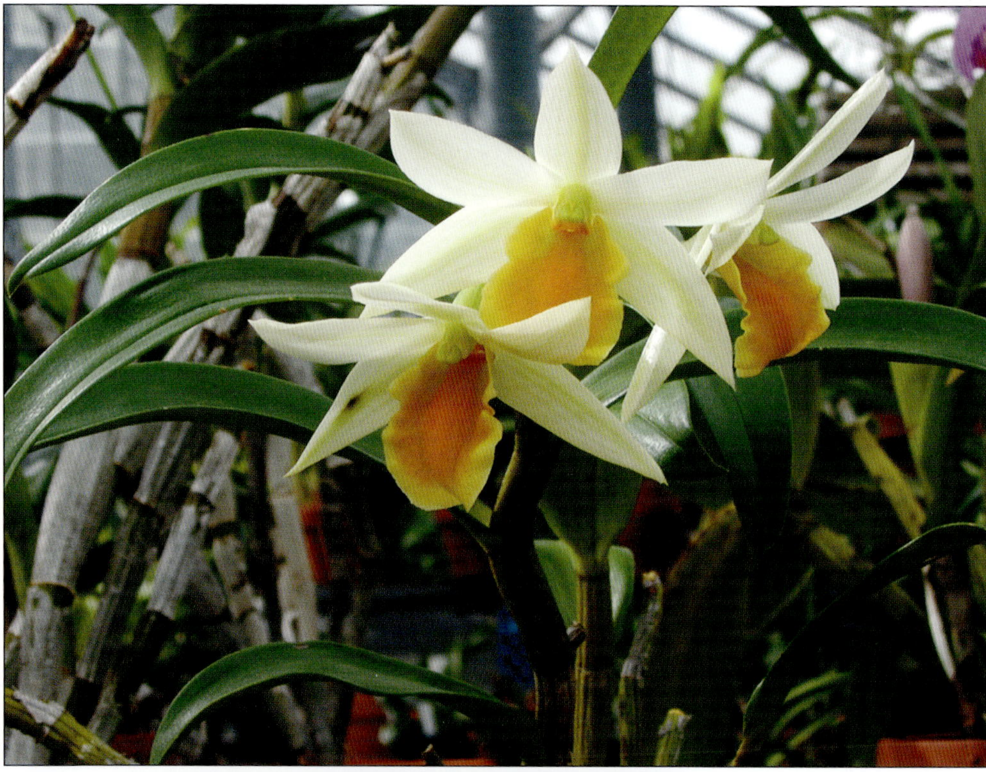

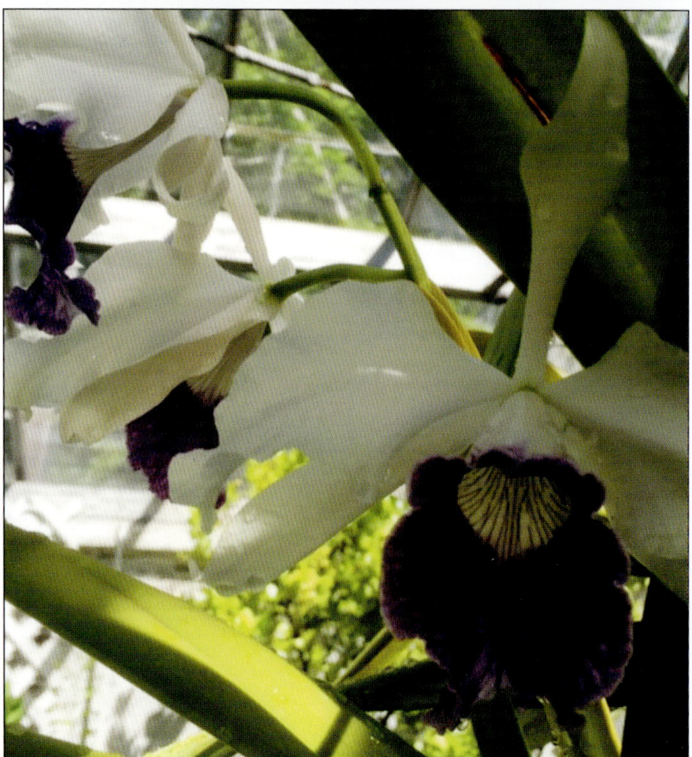

Orchid Collection. This collection has waxed and waned over the years, and while it lacks in number, it packs a punch in diversity and flowering. With as many as 15 genera in the late 1990s, the orchids represent both cool- and warm-loving plants. Many growth habits are represented, from upward growing *Phalaenopsis* to outward growers like *Cattleya*. Many in the collection are epiphytes, which grow on the trunks or branches of trees, not in the soil. Patience is required for the orchid grower. Some of the orchids have flowers lasting for months, while others only last for a few days.

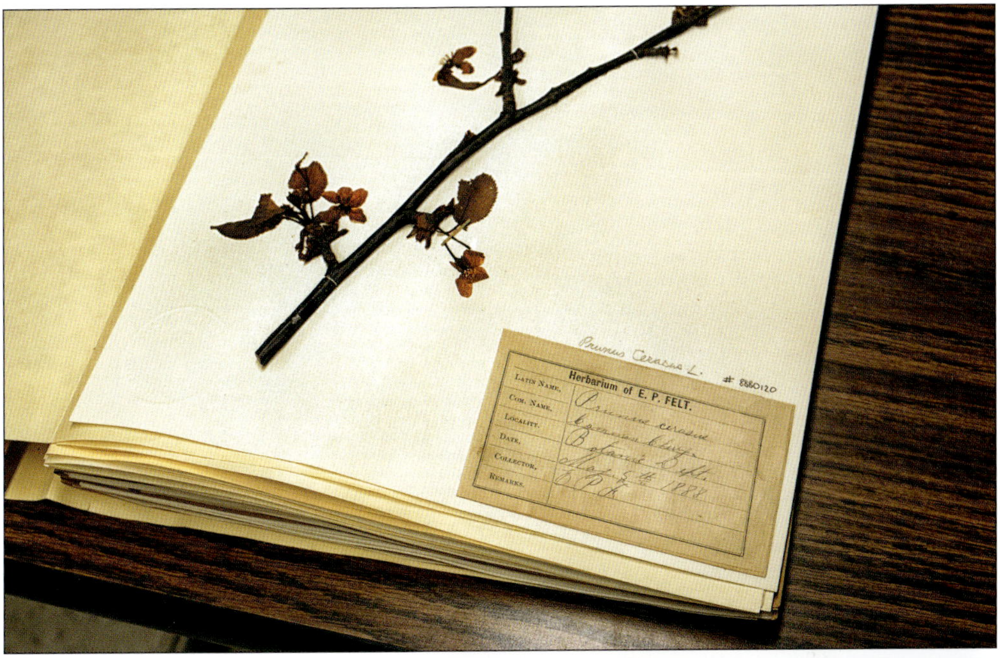

Herbarium. Not all of the collections at the arboretum are living. The Herbarium contains more than 7,500 specimens of vascular plants and bryophytes from throughout the world. The purpose of an herbarium is to make specimens from specific geographical locations or of a particular scientific interest accessible for scientific study and education. Branches, flowers, and seeds are mounted on sheets in a standardized method with detailed labeling, protected in folders, and filed in herbarium cabinets. Three hundred sheets of specimens in the arboretum collection dating to 1887 were created by E. Porter Felt, the first director and world shade tree authority at the Bartlett Tree Research Laboratories. Over the years, there have been gaps in the collection, but a renewed effort occurred in the 2000s, increasing the collection significantly. (Courtesy of Dan Lenore.)

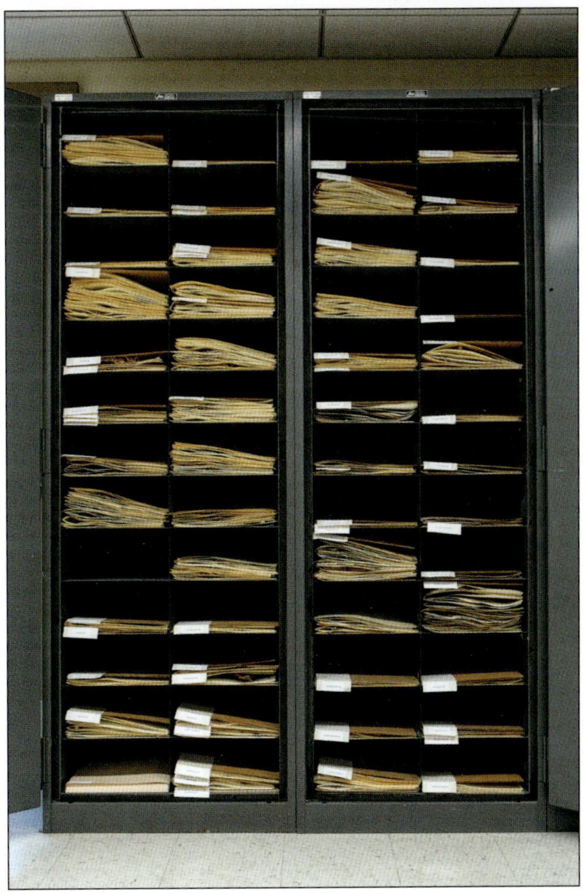

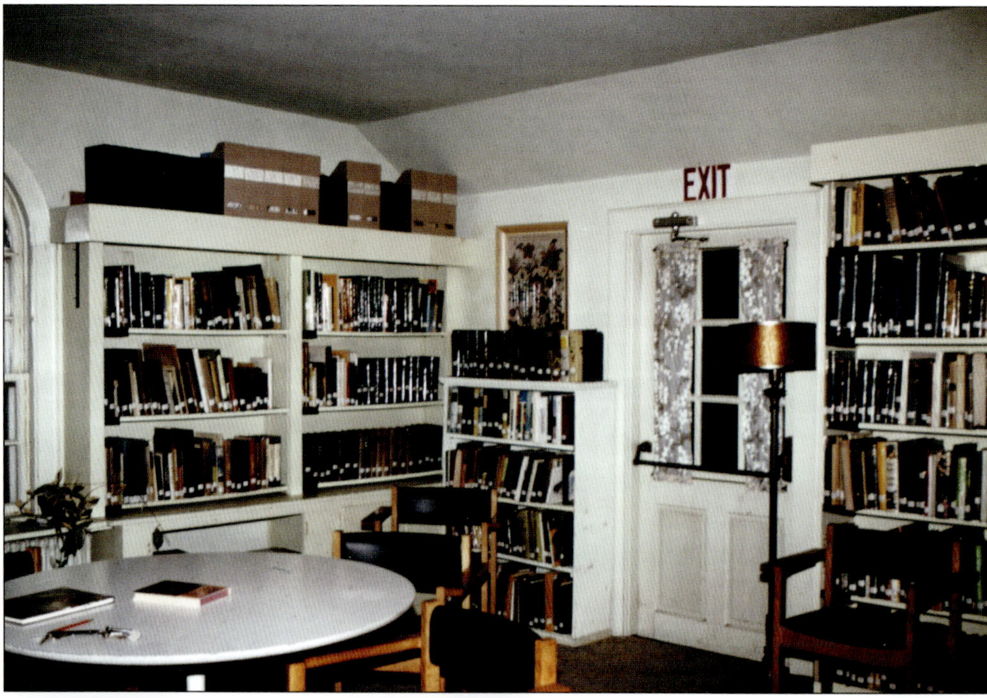

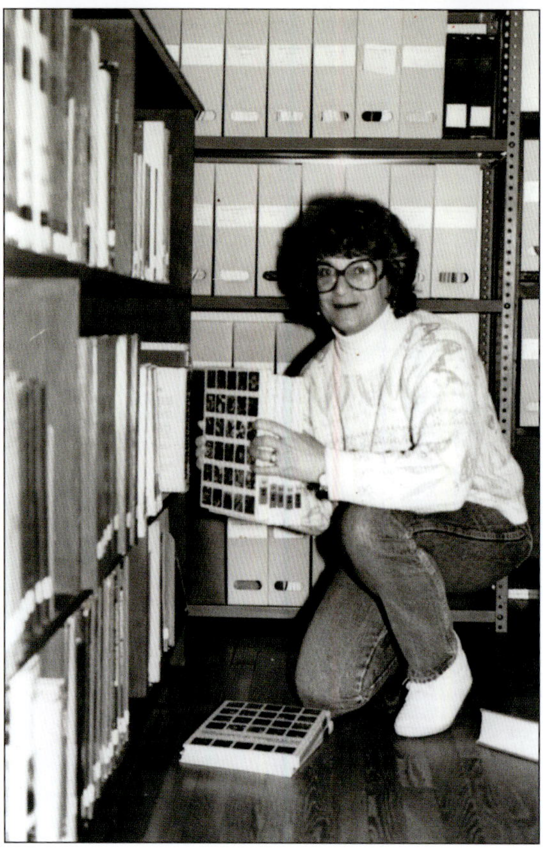

Horticultural Library Collection. Wanda Rogge is credited with first organizing the arboretum's extensive library collection in 1970. She created the best publicly available horticultural library in the state. In 1983, Leila Geronimo re-catalogued all the books to conform to the Dewey decimal system. In the spring of 1990, her work was updated by Pat Kotecki (left), who re-categorized each book according to the Library of Congress system and updated the card catalog. In the fall of 2000, Joan Soeth further updated the collection, which consists of books dating to the late 1800s. The library was originally housed in the Homestead in what was Dr. Bartlett's master bedroom (above).

Four

A Public Arboretum with Vounteers, Programs, and Events

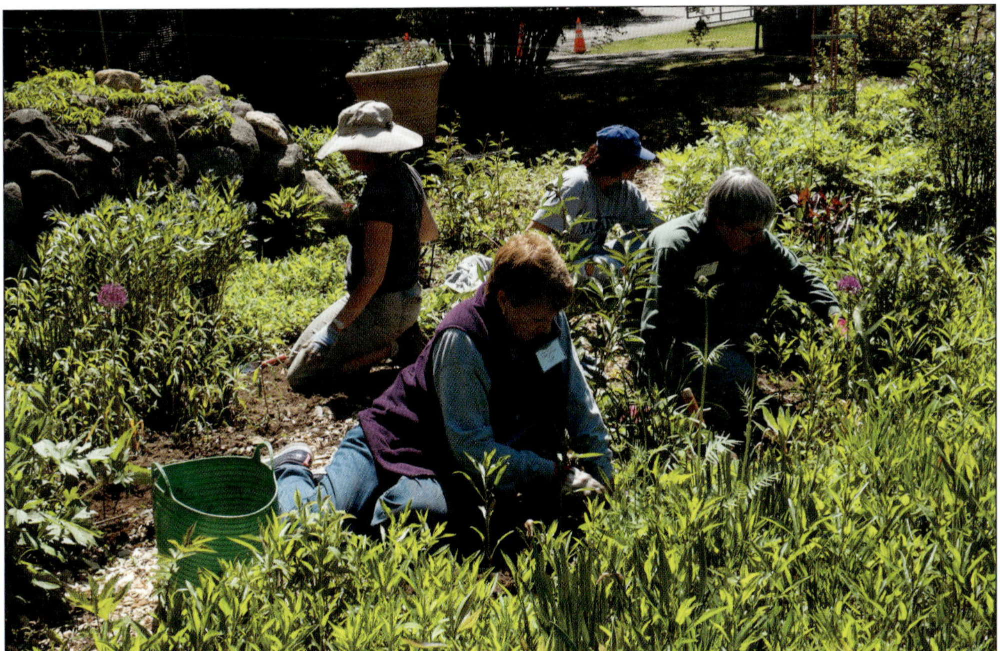

Expert Volunteers. Volunteers have always been the wheels that keep the arboretum going. Almost every day of the week, groups dedicated to certain gardens can be found toiling away. More than just weeders, they offer solid horticultural knowledge and expertise to the public; many have been certified as master gardeners, who do outreach in the community. (Courtesy of Dan Lenore.)

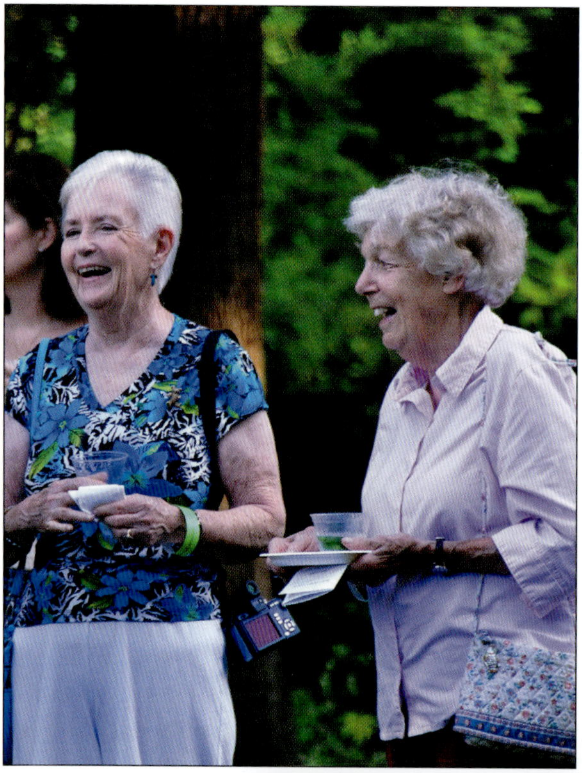

Longtime Volunteers. In 1985, the association elected Alice Smith (left, at right) and Carol Levine (below, at right) to the board. It is hard to picture the arboretum without these two, who together have performed decades of service and left an indelible mark on so many areas of the property. Both are formally trained in horticulture. Smith was the leader of the docent program (formerly Trail Guide program), and both were instrumental in establishing the Jane B. Heisinger Memorial Wild Flower Garden. Smith was also one of the originators of the Fern Allée with Phyllis Atkinson (left, at left). Levine is a popular lecturer about the wildflowers on the arboretum's trails and conducts botany identification walks year-round. Former board member Greg Moonie (below, at left) is a master composter, as well as a master gardener, and leads the docent program today.

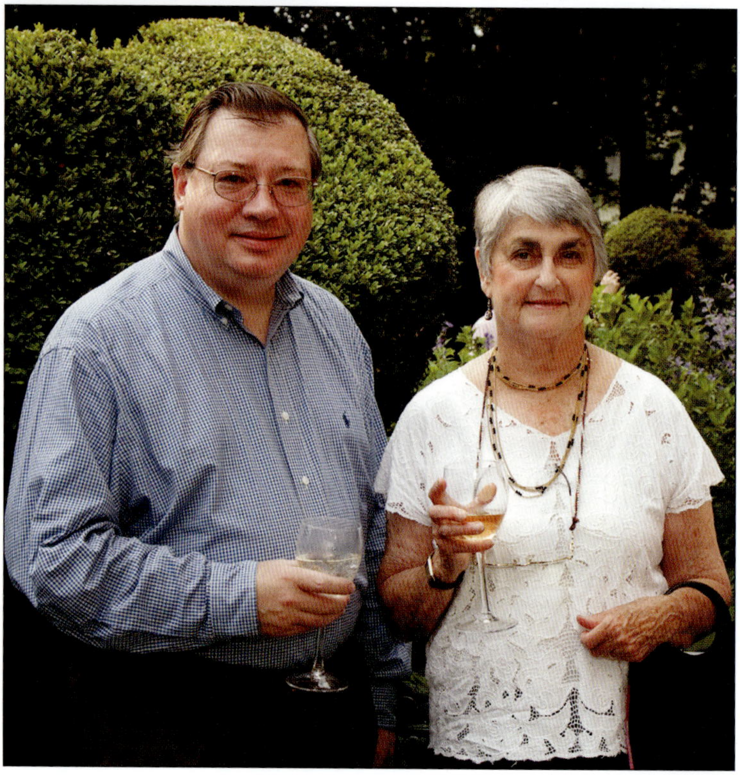

ROSE THIELENS. Rose Thielens helped initiate the Trail Guide program in 1969. Thielens died in 1990, leaving a bequest that was used to build a 27-station ecology walk with a printed guide. Stop No. 1 is called Boulder Fields, massive rocks rounded by the grinding of glacial ice during the last ice age. In 2016, the Rose Thielens Memorial Ecology Walk was renovated by Eagle Scout Aaron Jaffe, and the printed guide was digitized on the arboretum touring application.

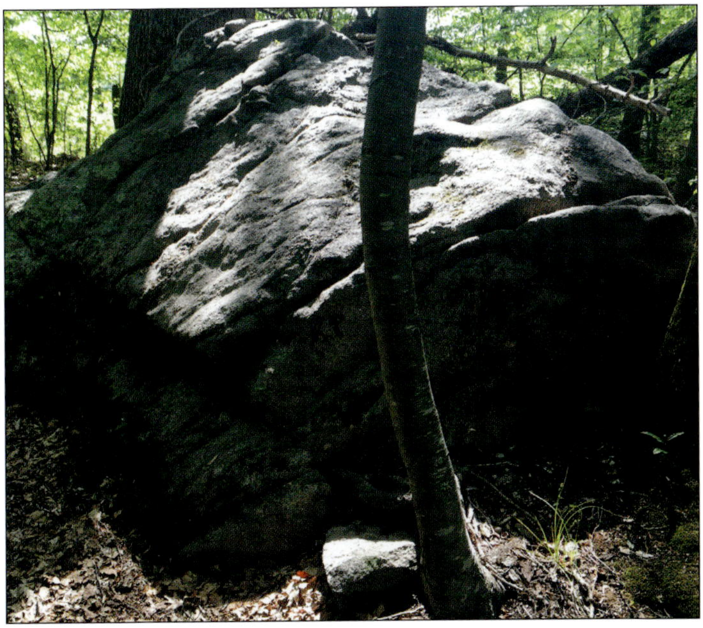

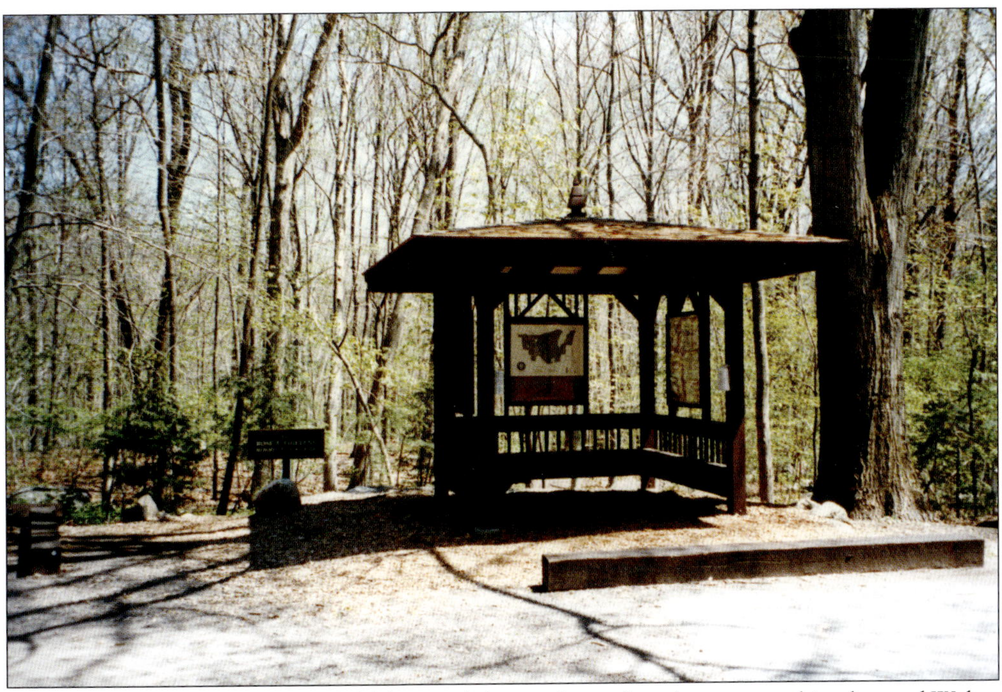

GREAT GAZEBO. In 1997, Ed Scofield designed the gazebo in the arboretum parking lot, and Walter L. Johnson, assisted by a group of dedicated volunteers known as the Monday Grounds Group, built it as a place to study trail maps and obtain educational materials. During the summer of 2016, a resurrection of the so-called "Great Gazebo" occurred when the deteriorated roof was rebuilt, once again with the help of volunteers.

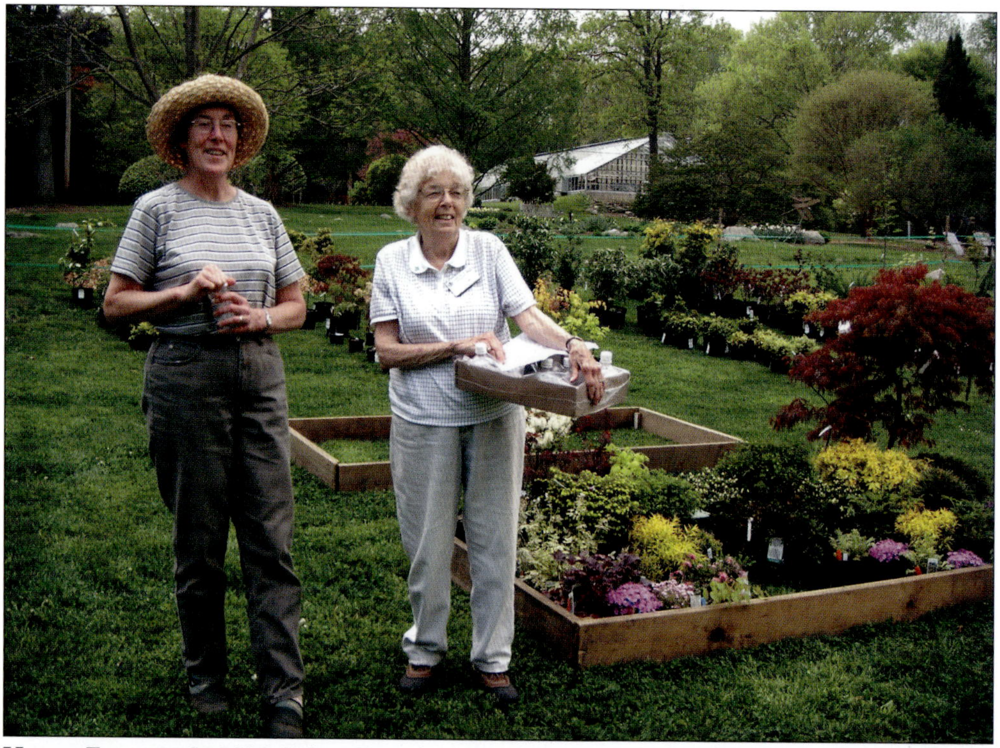

Hilary Forsyth. In 2000, Hilary Forsyth received the Volunteer of the Year award as "keeper of the Perennial Garden and ardent Plant Sale and Greenhouse volunteer." For the next 10 years, she was in charge of the Perennial Border, during which time she became a master gardener. Forsyth (left) and Alice Smith (right) wrote the foreword for this book.

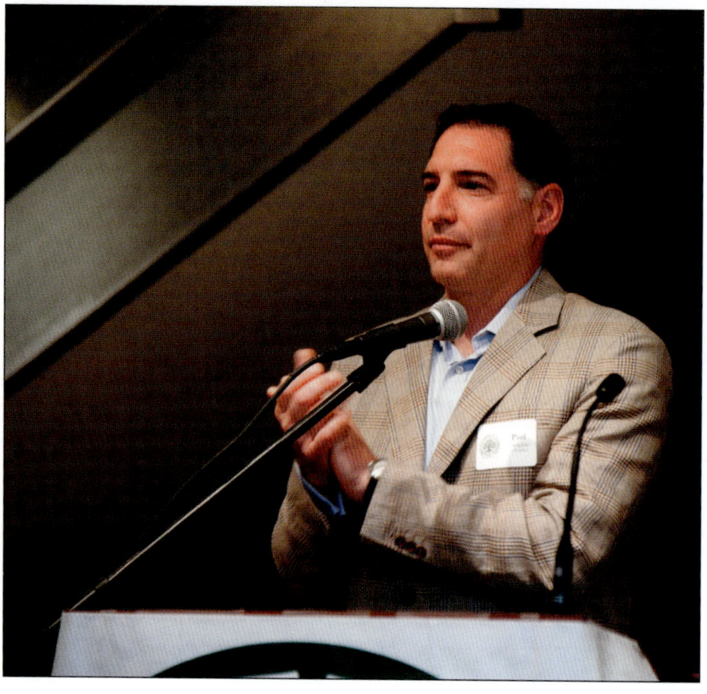

Paul Travaglino. Few will argue that the present-day angel of the arboretum is Paul Travaglino, who has tirelessly volunteered thousands of hours toward directing, planting, supporting, and guiding the arboretum through good times and challenging ones. He serves on the advisory committee and is an ex officio member of the board of directors as past president of the association, from 2012 through 2015. The arboretum is indebted to him for his dedication and selfless support.

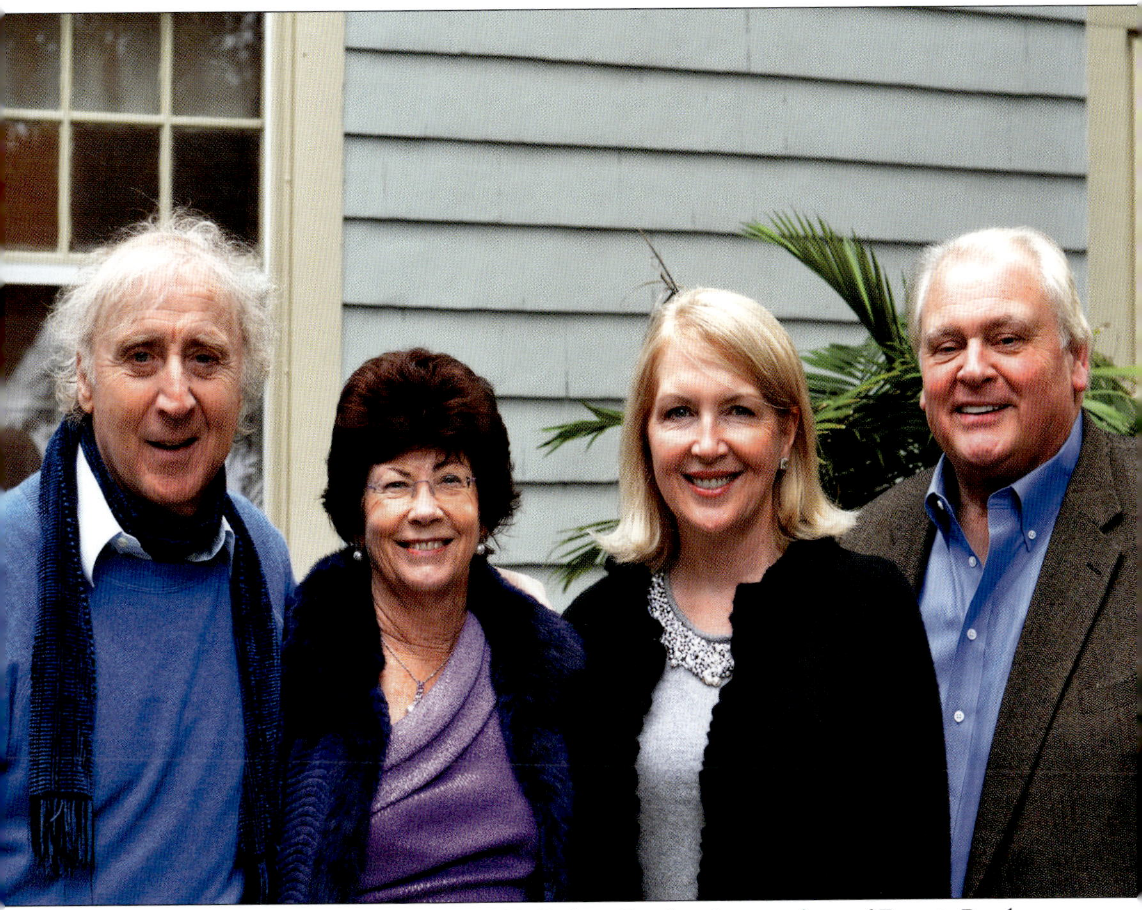

THE WILDERS AND THE BARTLETTS. In 1990, Robert Bartlett Jr., grandson of Francis Bartlett, became president of the Bartlett Arboretum Association. To this day, he is president of The F.A. Bartlett Tree Expert Company and makes his home in Stamford, Connecticut, where the home office of the company remains. He and his wife, Kate, have been loyal volunteers and donors for decades. In 2006, Kate Bartlett and Karen Wilder, wife of the late actor Gene Wilder, were chairs of the arboretum's 40th anniversary celebration, "An Evening in the Enchanted Forest." Karen Wilder led many arboretum events over the years. Kate, with arboretum neighbor Steve Watson, was the inspiration for the 2015 gala, "A Summer Féte." Robert Bartlett continues to support the arboretum through hundreds of hours of in-kind arboriculture work from The F.A. Bartlett Tree Expert Company. He is helping to lead the current expansion of the Conifer Garden and provided a generous challenge grant for guests at the 2016 gala to support the collections. The event's theme was "China in the Garden," a celebration of the arboretum's exotic plants, many of which his grandfather planted. From left to right are Gene and Karen Wilder and Kate and Robert Bartlett Jr.

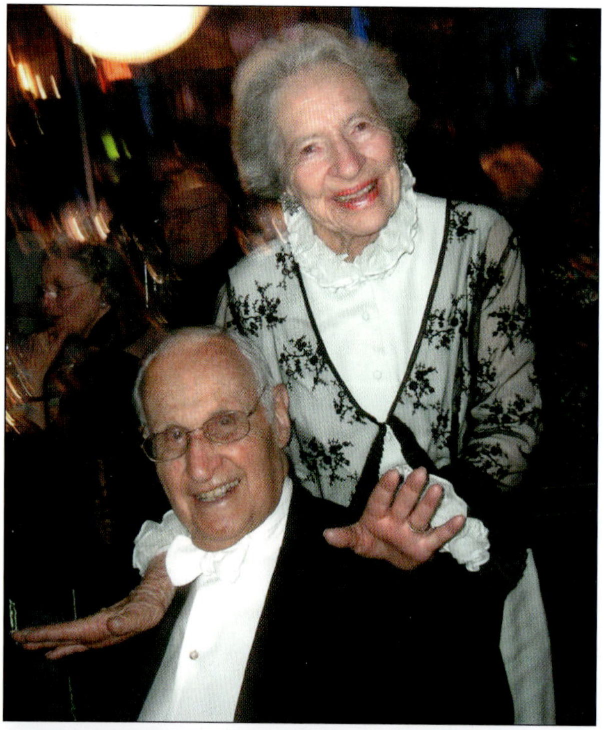

Edgar and Louise Cullman. Honorary chairs of the 40th anniversary celebration, Edgar and Louise Cullman are the largest monetary donors to date at the arboretum, giving a $500,000 gift supporting gardens, marketing, and development. Edgar Cullman, who owned General Cigar, was first and foremost a philanthropist. He died in 2011 at the age of 93, and Louise passed away in 2014.

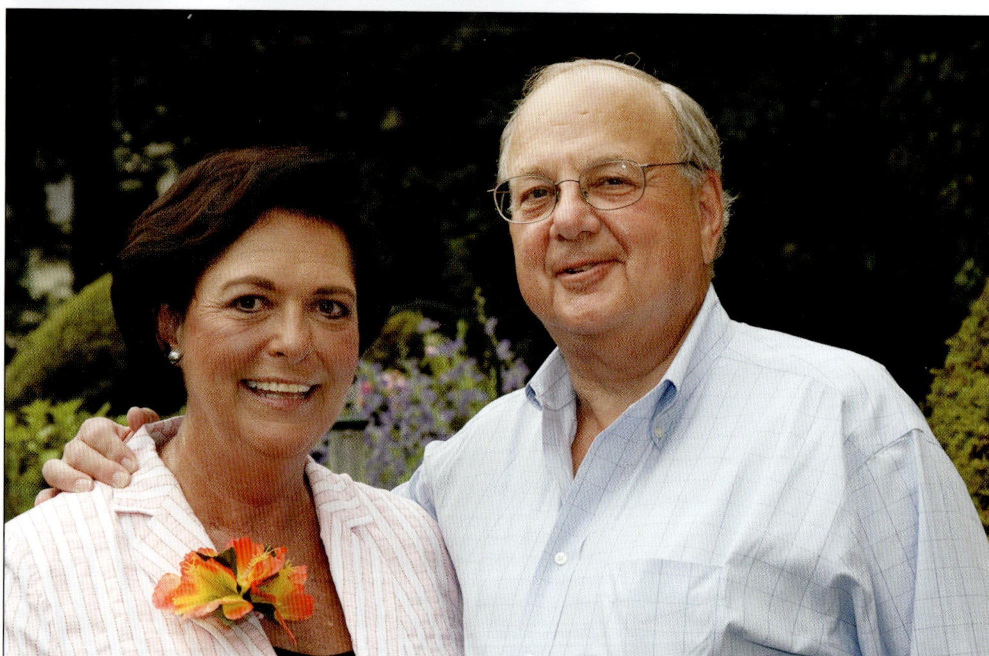

Vivienne and Richard Silver. Longtime supporters of economically disadvantaged children, the Silvers started a scholarship fund in 2004 to provide an exceptional day camp experience for children from Inspirica (formerly St. Luke's LifeWorks), a shelter for homeless families. The arboretum staff continues to include Inspirica campers with Richard Silver's support (Vivienne passed away in 2015). The Silvers donated $250,000 in 2011 to help build the Silver Educational Center.

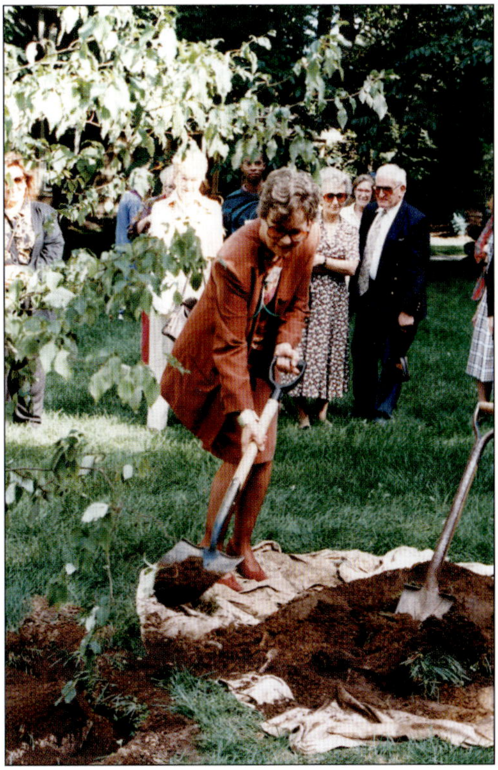

LONGEST EMPLOYEE. Many employees have come and gone, but few will argue that Gaye Mote is the most notable stalwart that the arboretum has ever known. She started her tenure in 1963 as a lab assistant and secretary for The F.A. Bartlett Tree Expert Company. She wore many hats after the state acquired the arboretum, remaining an employee for 31 years. She is pictured here retiring in 1998 and planting a tree. She worked as the first supervisor of the master gardener program, helped shelve and organize the first books in the library, worked in the plant clinic, wrote numerous articles for the newsletter, and served on several committees while running the arboretum as administrator.

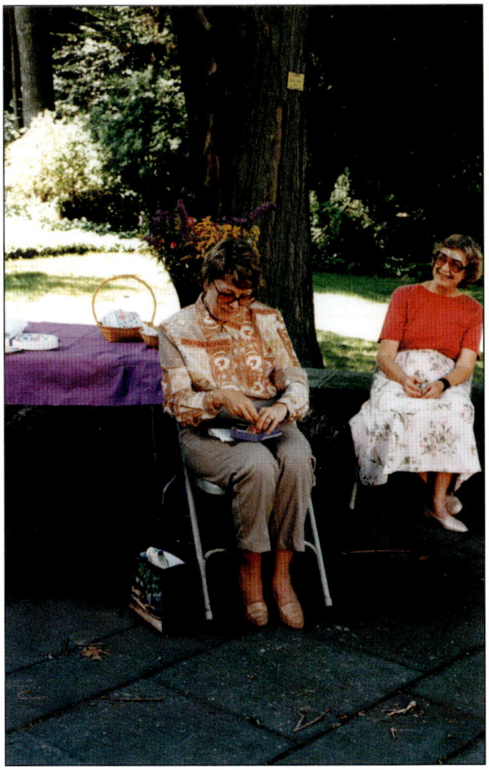

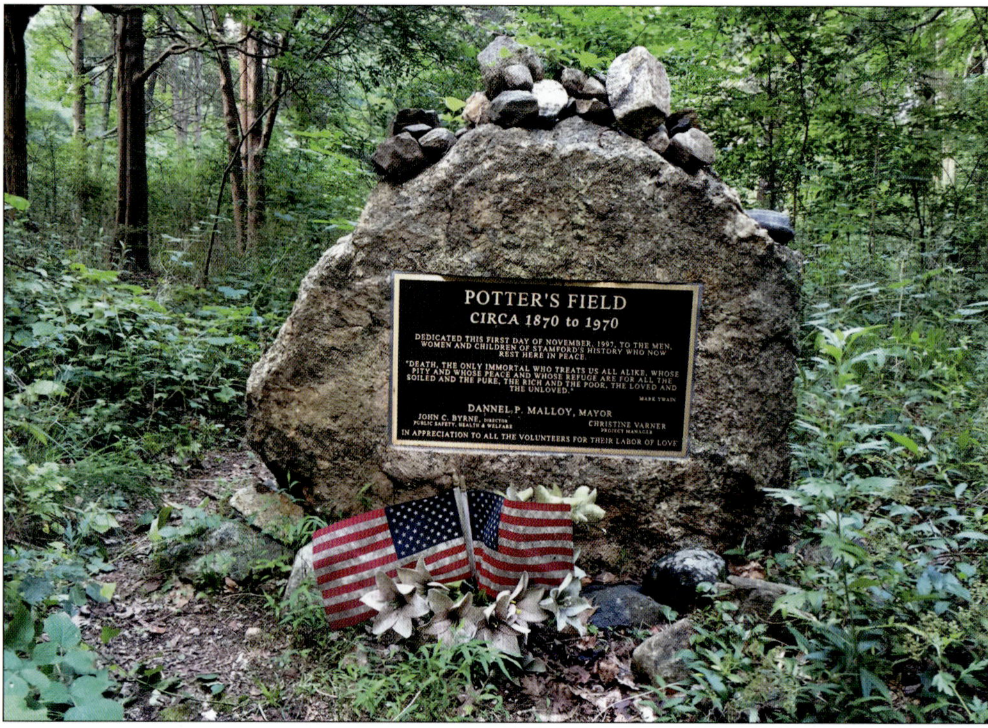

Potter's Field. When the City of Stamford became the proprietor of the arboretum, it added 27 more acres to the property, including an old cemetery where the city's indigents and late residents of the former poorhouse, Sunset House, were buried. Coincidently, it took 27 years for initial clean-up of the vine and brush entangled stones to commence, and in 1997, the 250-square-foot field buried with residents from around 1870 to 1970 finally received due respect. Employee Nick Pettit and the arboretum's director, Mark J. McDonnell, spearheaded the clean-up, and a former welfare director, Christine Varner, led the effort to identify 479 of those buried in Potter's Field. The cemetery was rededicated on All Saint's Day, November 1, 1997.

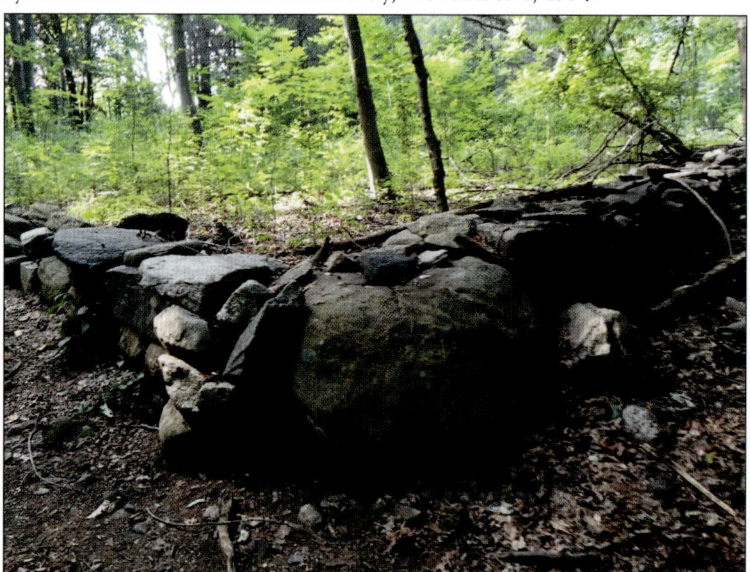

University of Connecticut Master Gardener Program. In 2001, the arboretum became one of the sites offering the state's extension certification program for master gardeners. Retiring in 2015 after 12 years of outstanding service, Regina Campfield coordinated the program, which provides staff for the plant clinic and helps maintain the gardens. They are the backbone of the volunteer workforce at the arboretum.

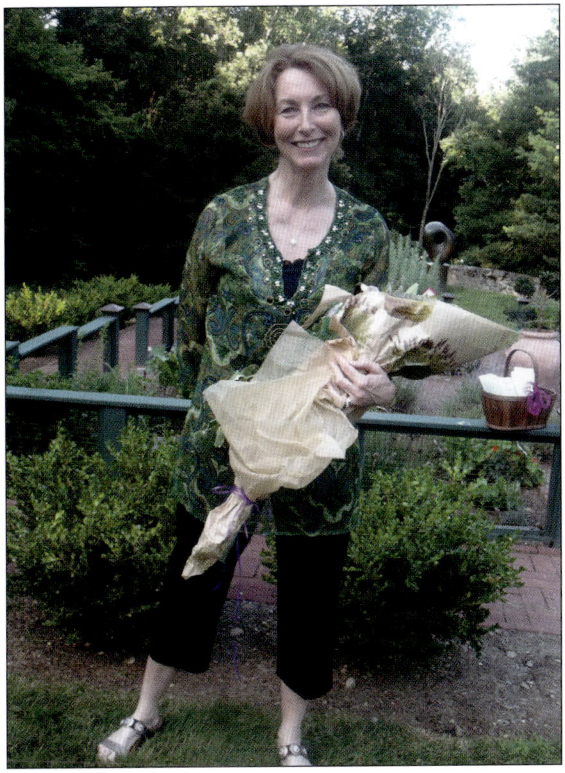

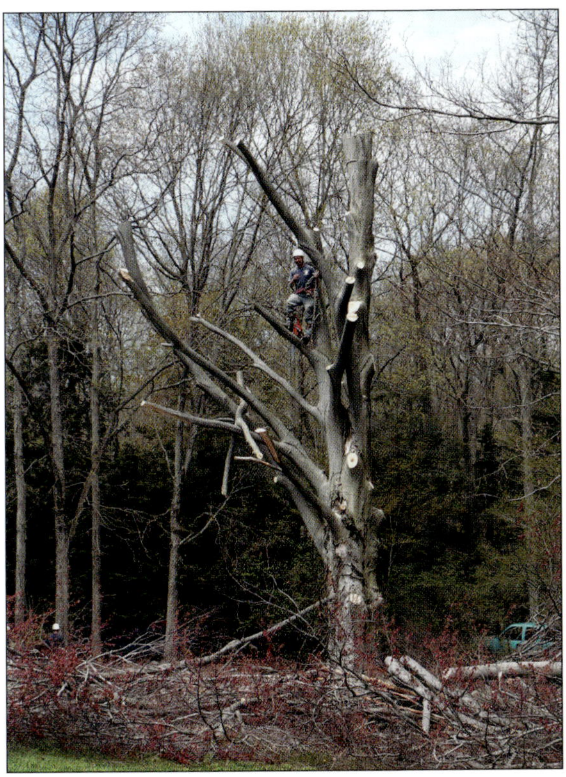

Professional Arborist Courses. True to Dr. Bartlett's mission, professional courses preparing individuals for the Connecticut arborist licensing exams are offered each winter. These courses, given in both Spanish and English, have been taught for the past 16 years by arborist David Tovar, who volunteers his time to ensure his pupils pass the rigorous tests required for certification.

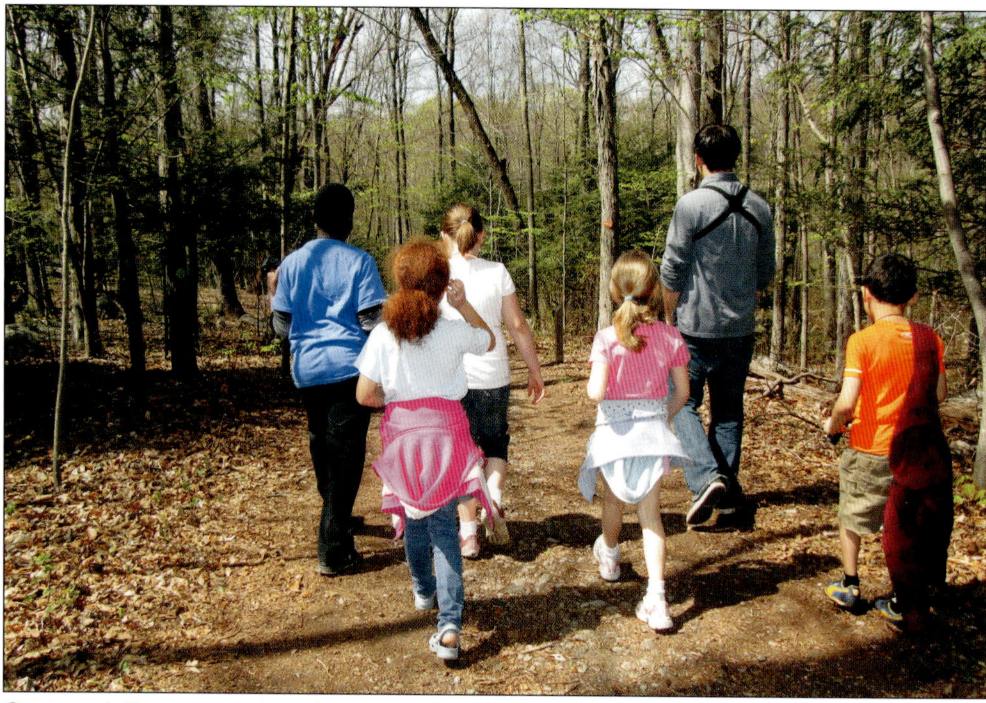

Children's Education. As early as 1989, the arboretum forged a relationship with Stamford Public Schools with a program called Project Learning Tree, in cooperation with the state Department of Environmental Protection. Originally led by educators from the state and professional naturalists, today's program has matured to encompass STEM (Science, Technology, Engineering, and Math) education and is taught by in-house environmental and botanical education specialists. The arboretum is visited twice a year by every public school second grader in Stamford to learn about seeds and flowering plants as part of their classroom science curriculum. Todd DuPont, children's education director from 2008 to 2016, took the program to the professional level it proffers today.

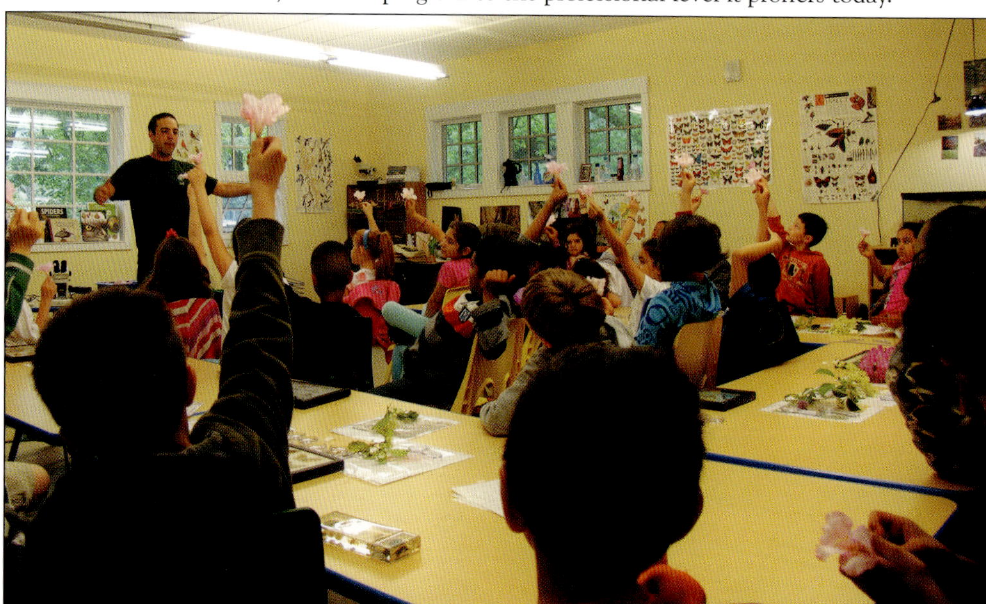

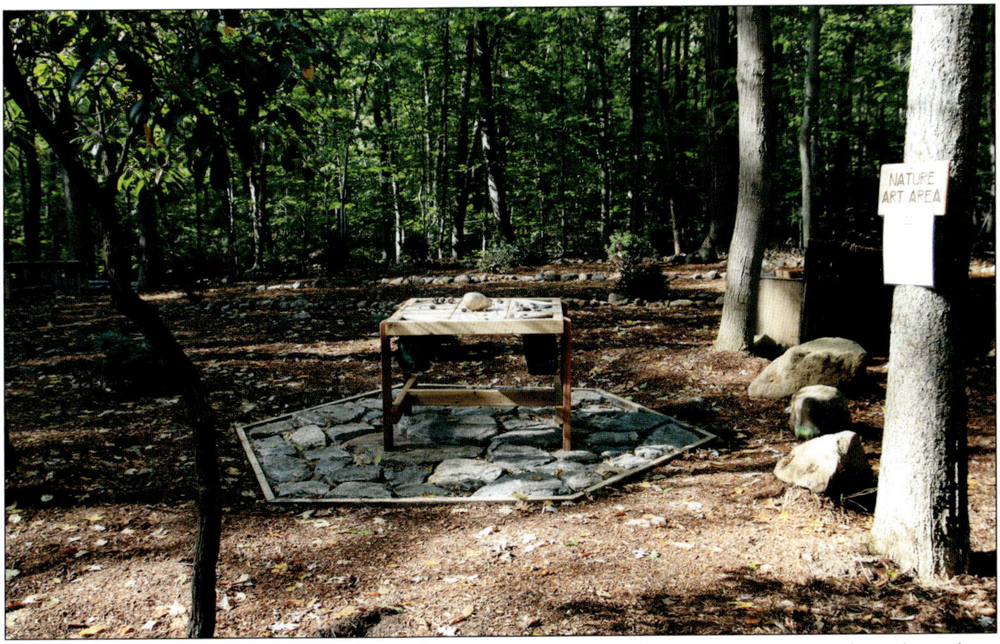

Nature Explore Classroom. The arboretum is the site of a dynamic nature-based outdoor interactive learning space near one of the trails in a wooded glen. The area has a stage, climbing apparatus, and two xylophones for musical creativity. The arboretum's camp and school groups use it for free play, as well as instructional environmental learning. The public is welcome to explore in this open and inspirational space. Constructed with grants from Keep America Beautiful and Pepsi Asia Network, it is kept play-worthy by several corporate groups, including Pitney Bowes, PricewaterhouseCoopers, and Nestlé Waters North America, which volunteer annually. (Below, courtesy of Nature Explore.)

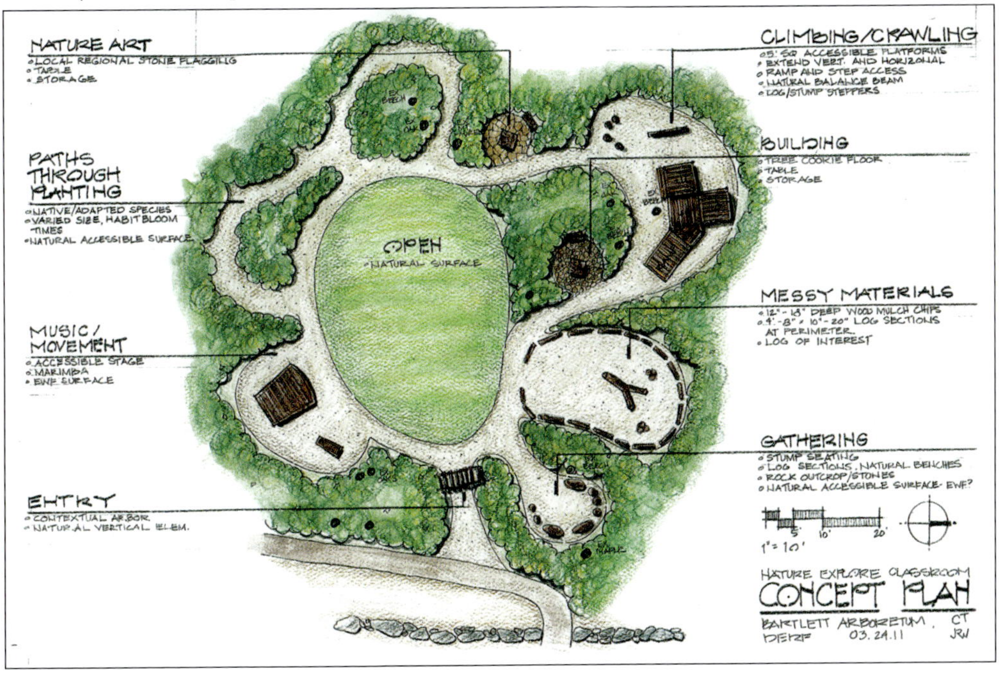

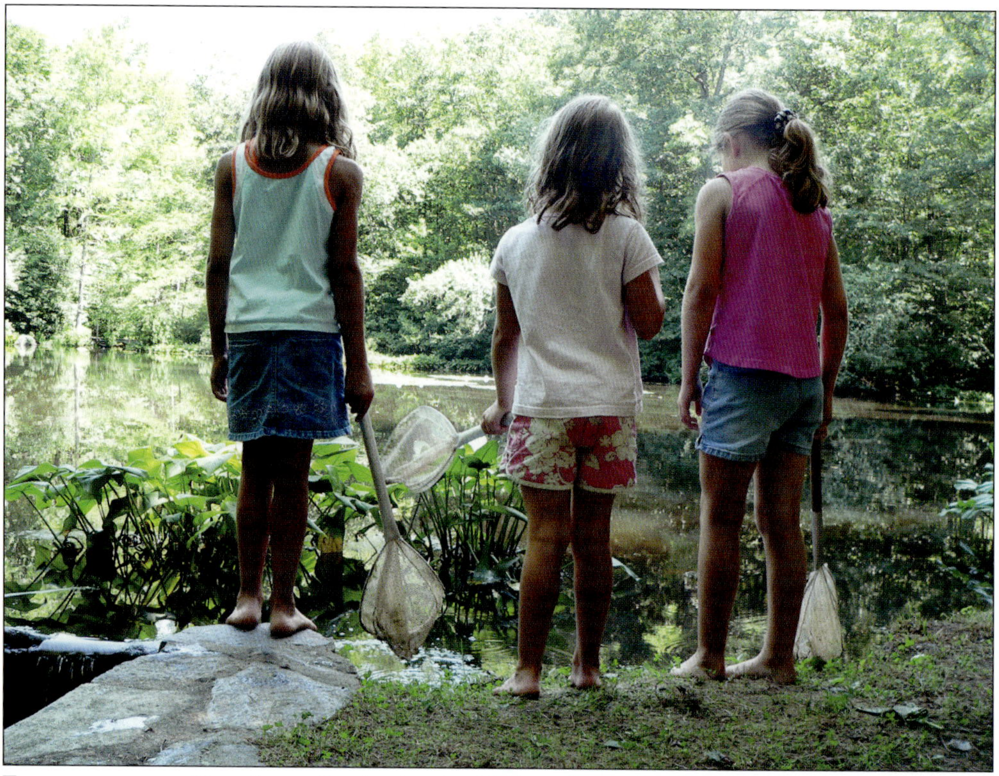

Environmental Day Camp. Beginning in 1997, early in the development of the children's education program, the arboretum hosted California-based Science Adventure, a summer day camp for kindergarten through sixth grade. By 2004, in-house educators soon realized that the arboretum had the resources and knowledge to offer its own program. From 2008 through 2016, Todd DuPont, director of children's education, masterminded a curriculum based on STEM subjects, incorporating art projects, storytelling, reading, and fun into scientific and botanical themes. Scholarship support from Richard Silver and others ensures that inner-city children, who would otherwise be unable to enjoy a rural summer respite, have access to the arboretum's quality, nature-based summer camp program.

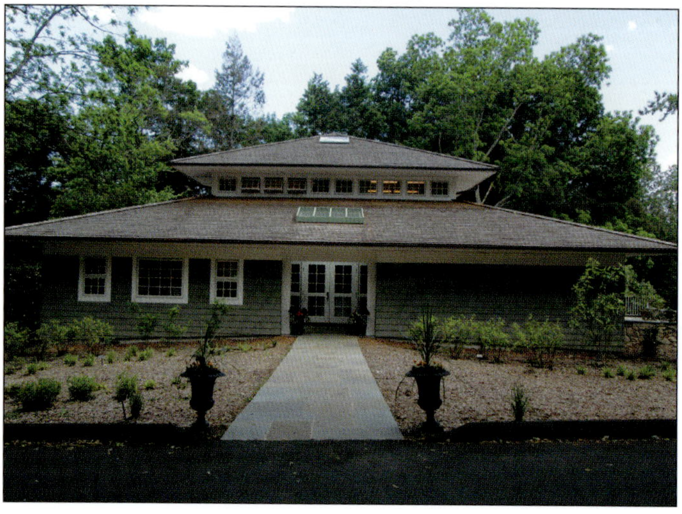

Silver Educational Center. The old Education Building, dubbed during the University of Connecticut years, served many generations of budding arborists as Stone Laboratories during Dr. Bartlett's time. It was time to replace the relic, and the City of Stamford and the Silver family offered the financial means to construct a new building in 2012 in the same general footprint of Stone.

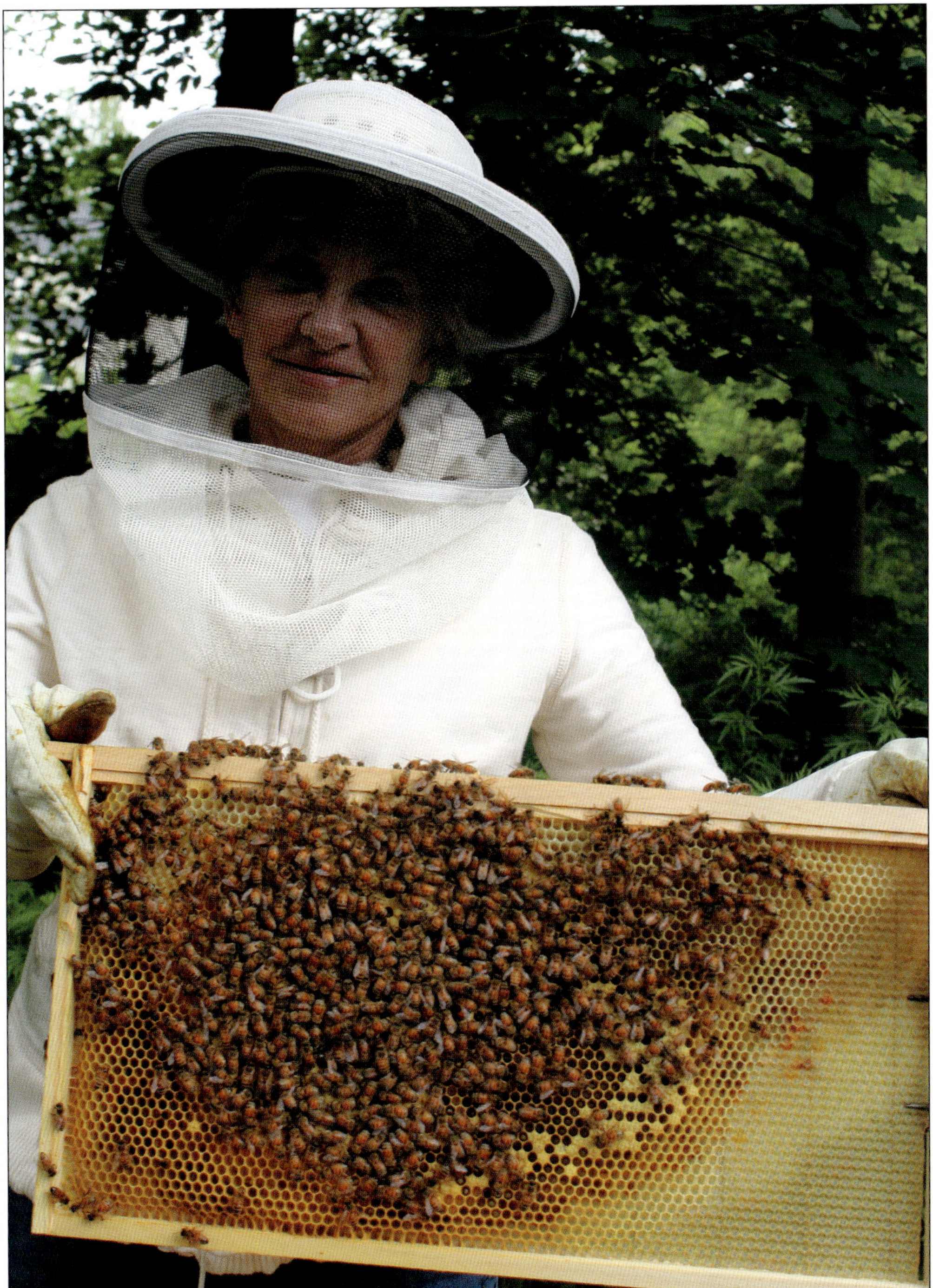

Cheryl Carter, Beekeeper. As early as 1977, the arboretum hosted beehives, enhancing the pollination of the diverse plant material on the property. Today, the arboretum's chief bee enthusiast is Cheryl Carter, who volunteers in many capacities, sweetest of which includes honey gatherer, hive relocator, and swarm protector. The hives serve as a natural educational tool for the children's programs and provide hundreds of pounds of honey for sale each year.

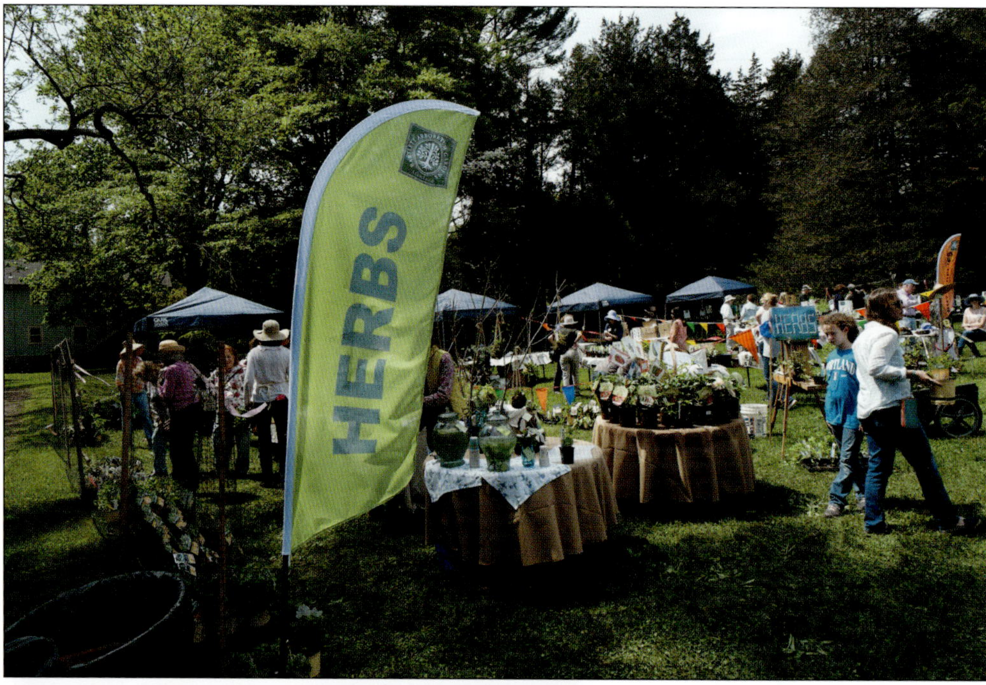

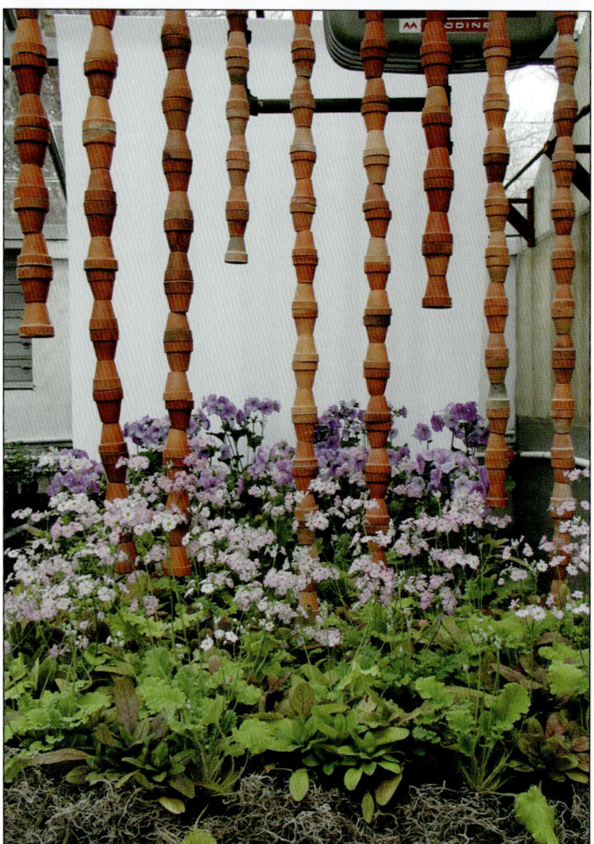

PLANT SALE. Initially established in 1981 and once called the Spring Garden Fair (in 1995), today's plant sale features native plants grown in the arboretum greenhouse. Vegetables, flowering perennials, herbs, and natives attract more than 200 visitors on sale day. At least 40 volunteers collect seeds, propagate, and care for the plants and then plan, set up, and sell plants during the plant sale, which augments the arboretum's budget each spring.

WINTER BLOOM. A glorious midwinter display staged in the greenhouse was first conceived as a way to brighten the dark days of winter. Planned and run by greenhouse volunteers, Winter Bloom became a full weekend of educational programs and exhibits by local nurseries and florists. As early as 1981, thousands of forced bulbs and flowering plants drew record visitors to the arboretum during the off-season.

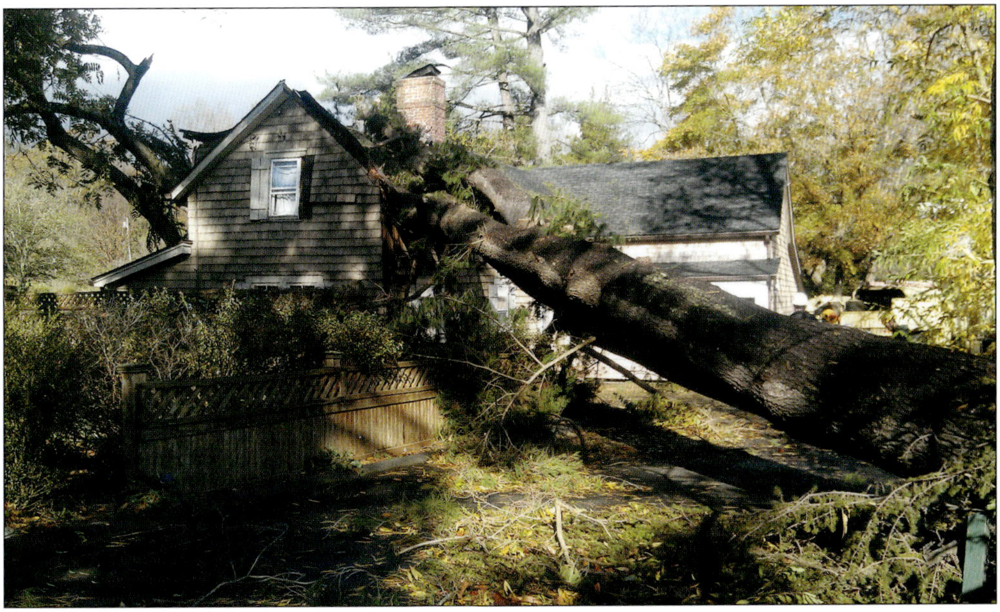

Stormy Weather. Hurricanes are inevitable in the Northeast and devastating for an arboretum. The arborteum reluctantly accepts the natural demise of trees, especially those planted more than 100 years ago by Dr. Bartlett, but the evidence of storms can be traced throughout the property by trees brought down long before their time. In 1986, Hurricane Gloria destroyed a specimen weeping Canada hemlock (*Tsuga canadensis* 'Pendula') and a unique upright growing pine (*Pinus strobus* 'Fastigiata'). One of Dr. Bartlett's prized heartnuts was fatally damaged as well. Hurricane Irene destroyed the original Bartlett chestnut, and Hurricane Sandy brought a giant white pine down on the 1934 cottage behind the Homestead, forcing it to be demolished in 2015.

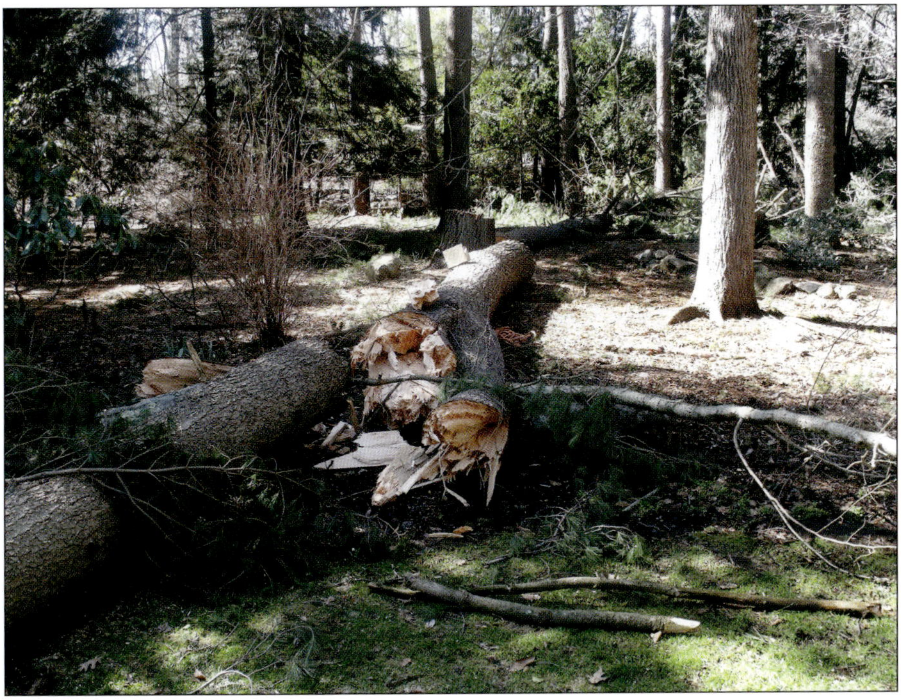

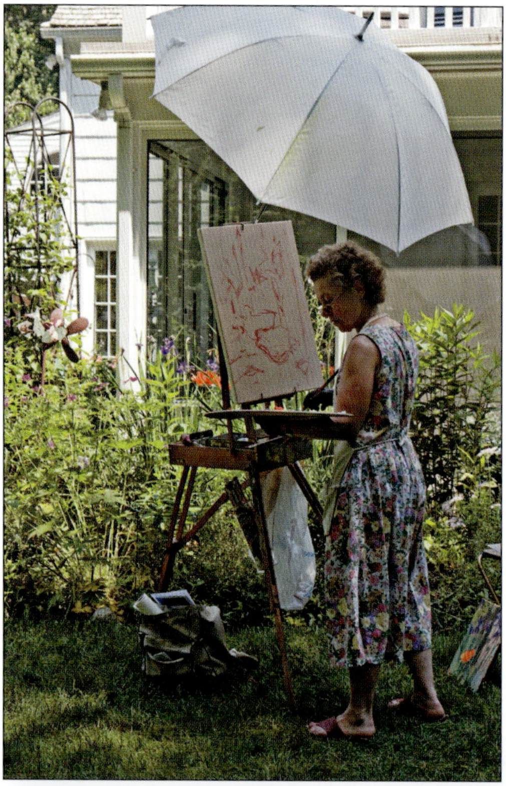

Arboreating and Garden Tour. Arboreating kicked off the fall season for many years with a festive gala, which served as a major fundraiser for the arboretum. One of the highlights of the spring season remains the spring Garden Tour, run by volunteers. Master gardener docents are stationed in area gardens chosen for their beauty and diversity, where they answer questions and impart their knowledge about the plants displayed in the gardens. Musicians serenade visitors who travel from garden to garden by car, and artists paint and/or photograph the gardens. Luncheon is served at the arboretum, the last stop on the tour.

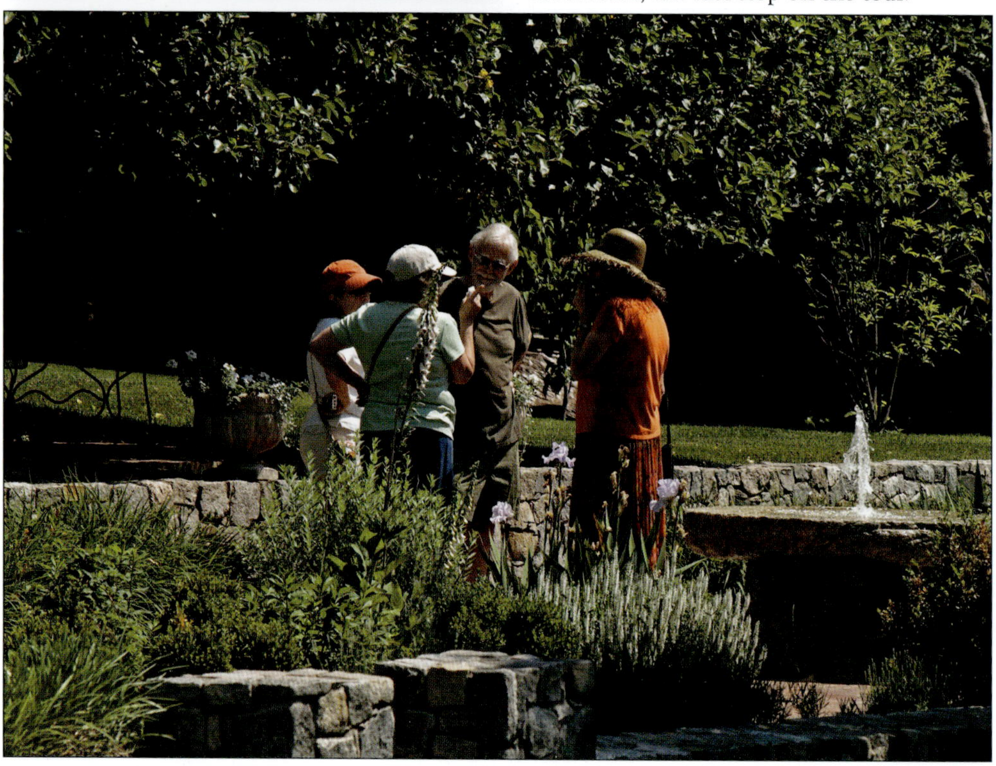

Designers' Showcase. The Homestead needed a long-overdue face-lift, and Sandy Paget (left) and Dianne Farley (right) became chairs of this event, which offered a unique solution: Open up each room to professional interior designers to show off their designs to the public as a fundraiser. Unique and splashy designs in each room attracted a large crowd during the weekend showcase. Following the event, further renovations overseen by Kate Bartlett and interior designer Steve Watson furnished the Homestead beautifully for use as administrative offices, as well as for event rentals. Part of the original showcase work, the walls climbing the staircase are hand-painted.

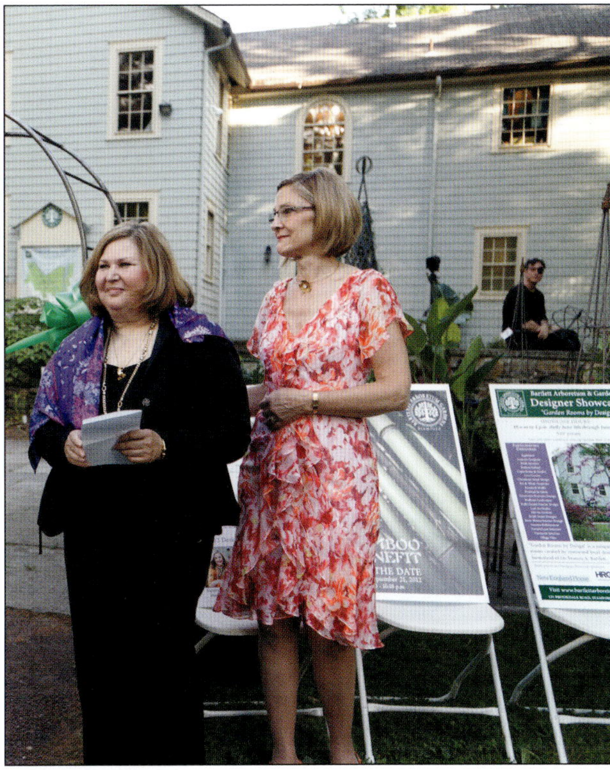

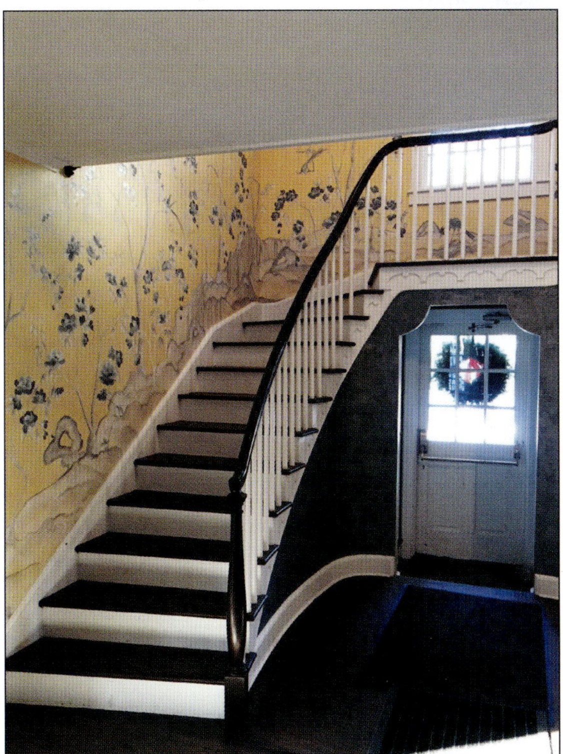

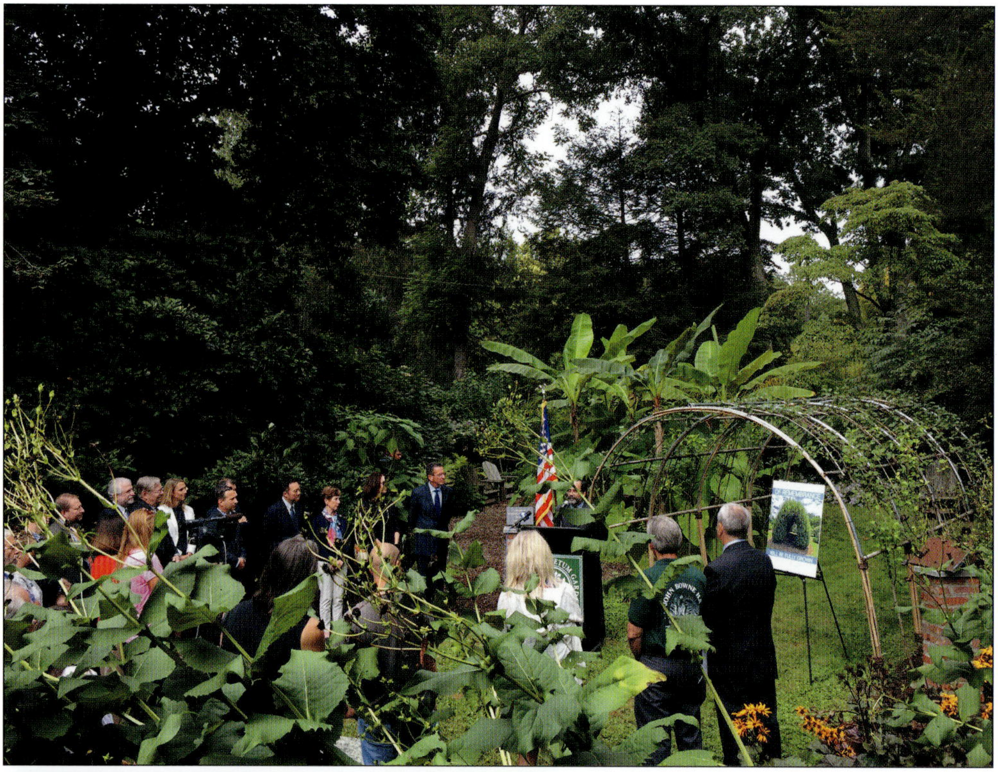

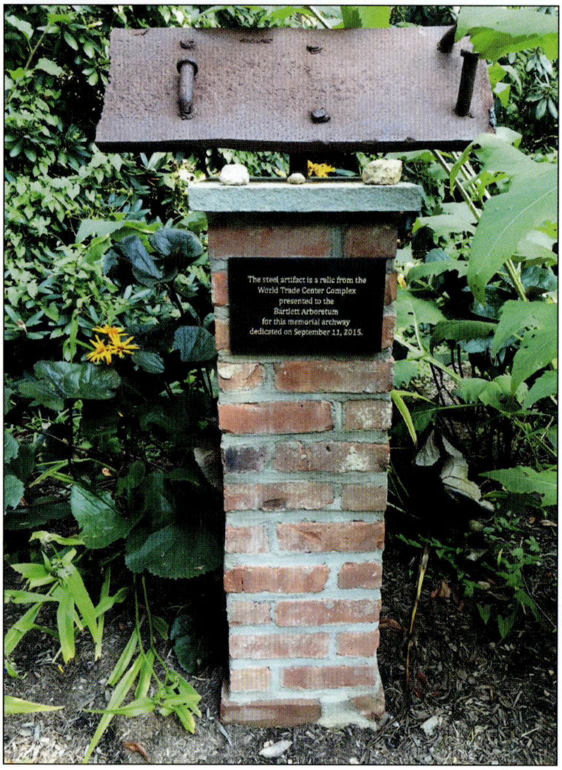

9/11 Memorial Archway. On September 11, 2015, a living memorial was dedicated in the Secluded Garden to those who lost their lives during the attacks on the World Trade Center in New York City. The "Survivor Tree," a Bradford callery pear (*Pyrus calleriana* 'Bradford'), was found alive in the rubble and replanted at the National September 11 Memorial & Museum. Students from John Bowne High School in Flushing, Queens, took cuttings from the tree, 14 of which were planted in a memorial archway on the arboretum property. Connecticut governor Dannel Malloy and Stamford mayor David Martin, along with other dignitaries, attended the dedication. An artifact from the rubble is mounted near the archway.

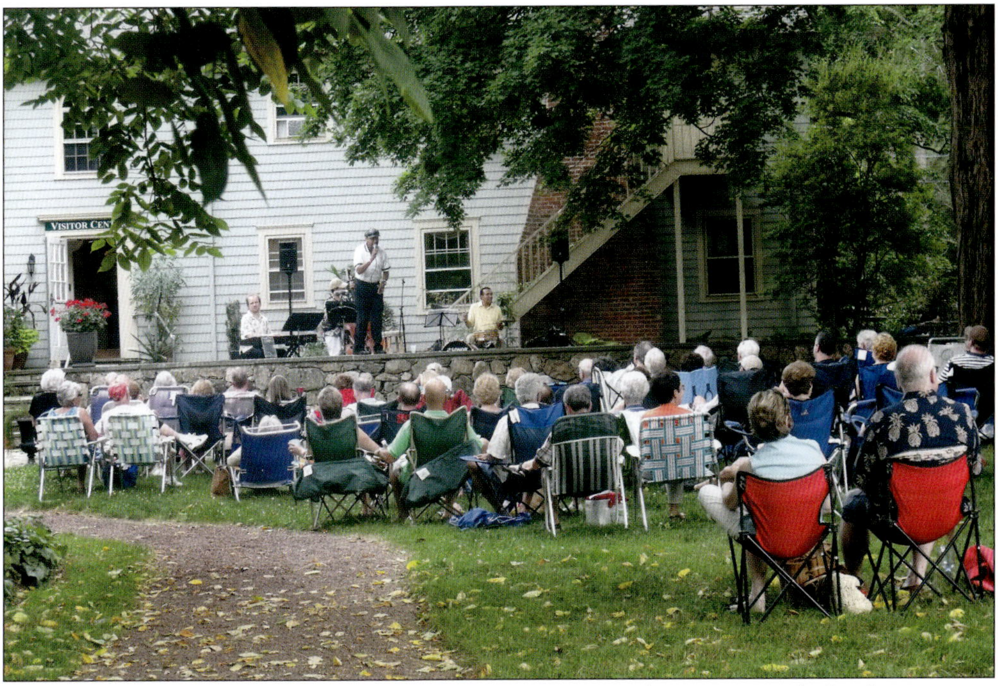

Summer Concerts. In 1994, free summer concerts were initiated to encourage the local community to visit and enjoy the many resources the arboretum has to offer. The first bands, the South Avenue Society Jazz Band, Norfield Woodwind Quintet, Stamford Master Singers, and Prevailing Winds Quintet, laid the groundwork for today's morning classical and afternoon mixed genres of folk, bluegrass, pop, and rock. While a nominal fee is charged now, the same sense of community is felt as picnickers spread out over the lawns and enjoy the music played on the Homestead patio on Sundays.

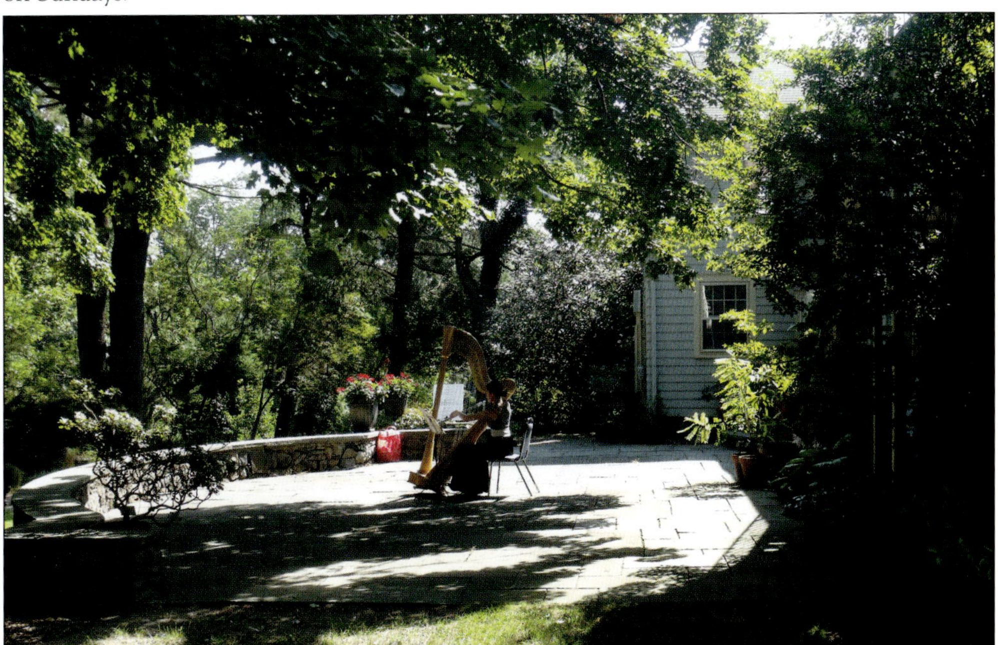

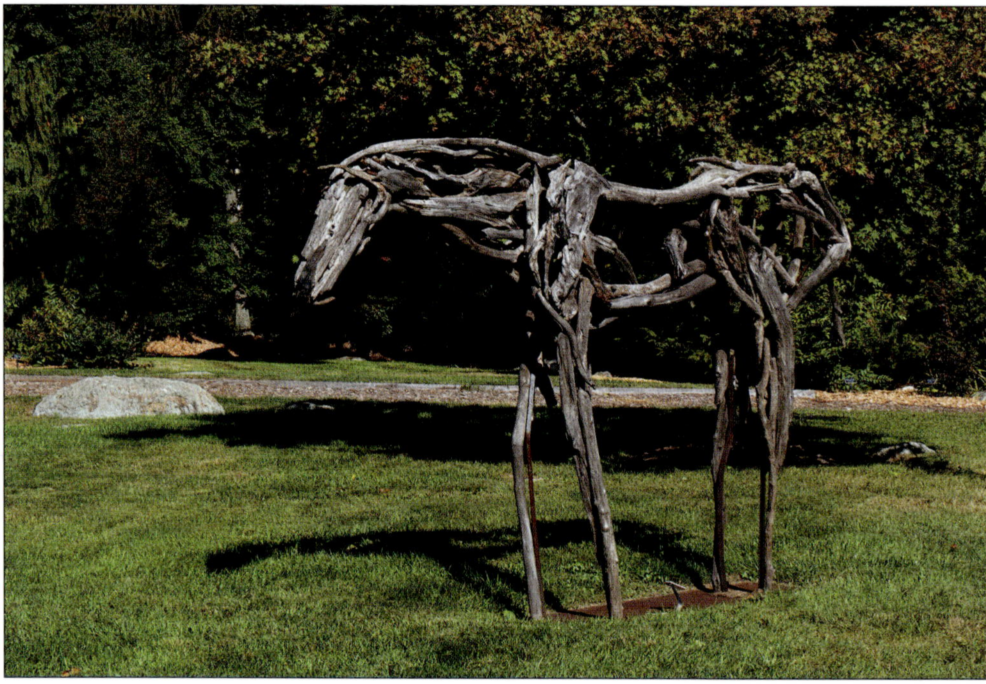

Art Exhibits. For decades, the arboretum has hung special art exhibits in various buildings and displayed sculpture in the gardens. It is a favorite venue for en plein air artists, who find inspiration in the natural beauty of the gardens, meadows, and woodlands. Art classes meet weekly year-round in the Silver Educational Center, which offers perfect natural lighting for all genres of art—watercolor, oil, acrylic, and photography. In 2015, an alliance was formed with the Stamford Loft Artists Association, with new local artists' works put on display every few months, starting with a wine and cheese opening event.

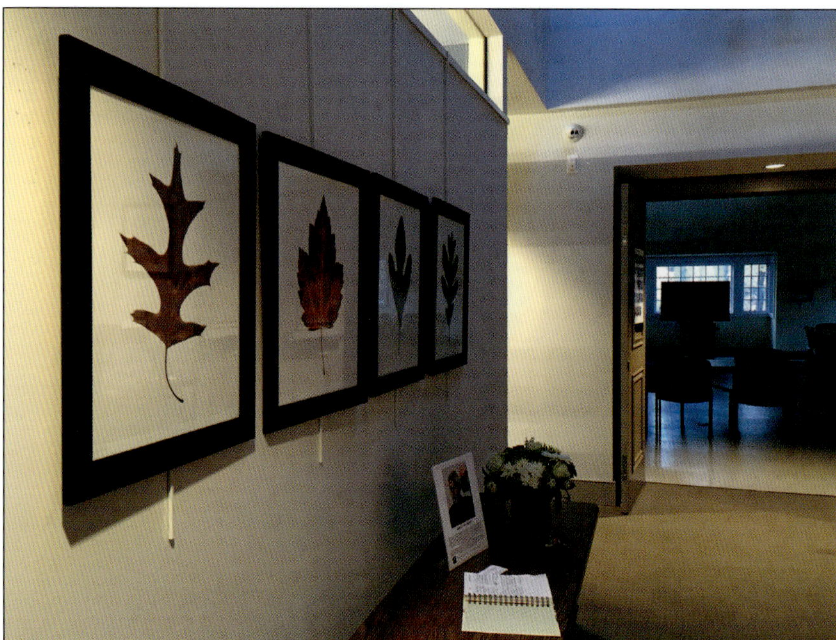

BIBLIOGRAPHY

"A Reverence for Wood." *Stamford Advocate*. December 20, 1965.

Bartlett Arboretum News, published seasonally from Spring 1978–Summer 2006.

Cooley, Laurel B. *The Bartlett Way*. Stamford, CT: The F.A. Bartlett Tree Expert Company, 2007.

Dirr, Michael. *Manual of Woody Landscape Plants*. Champaign, IL: Stipes Publishing Company, 1990.

Gerhold, Henry D., and Stacy A. Frank. *Our Heritage of Community Trees*. Mechanicsburg, PA: Pennsylvania Urban & Community Forestry Council, 2002.

Strogoff, Erin. "Connecticut's 'The Legend of the Charter Oak.'" Connecticut Public Broadcasting Network and Connecticut Historical Society. This article originally appeared on *Your Public Media*.

"Transfer Action Completed for Bartlett Tract." *Stamford Advocate*. November 23, 1965.